PRIMARY DOCUMENTS of 20TH CENTURY CANADA

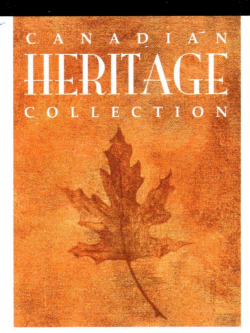

CANADIAN HERITAGE COLLECTION

CITIZENSHIP AND GOVERNMENT

Rick Homan

Series Editor
Don Kendal

Rubicon

To Yvonne for her patience. Rick

Rubicon © 2004 Rubicon Education Inc.

Editorial Coordinator:	Martine Quibell
Project Editors:	Miriam Bardswich, Kim Koh
Design:	Jennifer Drew
Assistant Designer:	Jeanette Debusschere

All rights reserved. No part of this publication may be reproduced, stored in a database or retrieval system, distributed, or transmitted in any form or by any means, electronic, mechanical, photocopying, recording, or otherwise, without the prior written permission of the Publisher.

Every reasonable effort has been made to acquire permission for copyright material used in this book. Any errors or omissions called to the Publisher's attention will be corrected in future printings.

National Library of Canada Cataloguing in Publication

Homan, Rick
    Citizenship and government / Rick Homan.

(Canadian heritage collection)
Includes bibliographical references and index.
ISBN 0-921156-77-4

    1. Canada--Politics and government—Textbooks. 2. Citizenship—Canada—textbooks. 3. Civics, Canada—Textbooks. I. Title.
II. Series: Canadian heritage collection (Oakville, Ont.)

JL187.H65 2003   320.971   C2003-900353-1

Printed in Canada

COVER:

Kirsty Ross *(left),* and Nicola Fahey display
a handful of Canadian flags, 23 July 2002.
(CP PHOTO/Andrew Vaughan)

Table of Contents

Introduction	4
1860 – 1869	6
1870 – 1899	10
1900 – 1919	14
1920 – 1929	18
1930 – 1939	20
1940 – 1949	24
1950 – 1959	28
1960 – 1969	30
1970 – 1979	34
1980 – 1989	38
1990 – 1999	42
Into the 21st Century	46
Index	48

INTRODUCTION

> "Nature endowed us with a magnificent setting, our ancestors developed an impressive culture; let every man, woman and child use the democratic process to contribute to the creation of one Canada."
>
> — Lorry Greenberg, Mayor of Ottawa

CANADA BEGAN AS A CONSTITUTIONAL compromise and has often been described as "ungovernable," yet it has one of the world's most stable political systems. Furthermore, Canada has a diverse, multicultural population within an officially bilingual framework that recognizes the original deal struck between the French and English founders.

Canada's respect for multiculturalism gives it a unique identity. However, it has not always been that way. Many minorities have been discriminated against and have had to struggle to achieve equality. For example, at the turn of the 20th century, Chinese workers were encouraged to immigrate to Western Canada as cheap labour to build the railroad. However, when the economy took one of its many cyclical downturns, these same immigrants were accused of taking jobs from white Canadians. As a result, immigration was cut off and a discriminatory "head-tax" was imposed on prospective Chinese immigrants.

First Nations people have also faced discrimination in Canada. A long history of ill-treatment includes long-disregarded treaty rights and land claims, human rights and other abuses in residential schools, extreme poverty on many reserves, and the existence of the paternalistic Indian Act.

Canada today is much different from the Canada established by the Fathers of Confederation in 1867. It took time, imagination, deal-making, and practical solutions to local problems to convince the outlying colonies to join the original four in the young Dominion. Western expanses, purchased from the Hudson's Bay Company, were brought into Confederation with promises to build a railroad and to protect Métis culture and religion. Eastward expansion of the Dominion depended on federal government support payments to help the Atlantic colonies deal with their debts.

The new Dominion of Canada was brought into being with the passage of the British North America Act by the British Parliament in London. The governing structure had five essential components: a democratically-elected government, a constitutional monarchy, a federal system, political parties, and protection of the rights of citizens through the rule of law.

First, the democratically-elected government is accountable to the citizens by being answerable to their elected representatives in Parliament for all its decisions. Ultimately, if the people do not like those decisions, they can choose a new government in the next election, which has to occur at least every five years.

However, at the time of Confederation, Canadian democracy was not all that democratic. Initially, only men who were British subjects could vote or hold public office. The 1900 Dominion Elections Act made it clear that many visible minorities, women, and First Nations people would not be allowed to vote. Some women got the federal vote in 1918, the rest in 1920. By 1948, Chinese- and Japanese-Canadians were guaranteed the right to vote, but not all Native Canadians living on reserves got the franchise until 1960.

Secondly, Canada is a constitutional monarchy. The British monarch is also the King or Queen of Canada. The Governor General fulfills the monarchy's primarily symbolic role as the official Head of State.

Thirdly, the Fathers of Confederation established a federal system that divided the many responsibilities of the government between the new federal administration and the governments of former colonies and the newly-created provinces. Each level of government was granted exclusive jurisdiction over areas that more directly affected them. Both levels shared some powers. The federal government was left with control over any issues that emerged over time and was to prevail in situations where the powers of both levels of government conflicted. Local government was not recognized as a separate, third level of government. Therefore, towns and cities remain under the control of the provinces.

Political parties emerged to represent the differing views of Canadian citizens. Elections are technically meant to allow citizens within each constituency the opportunity to choose one individual to represent them in Parliament. In practice, each candidate, with some notable exceptions, represents the views of a political party led by someone who is also a candidate for election in a separate constituency. In most cases, the party that has the most representatives elected becomes the party in power, and its leader becomes the Prime Minister or provincial premier. The Prime Minister then selects the government (the Cabinet ministers) from among those party members who were successful in getting elected in their own constituencies. Elected members of the government party who are not in Cabinet are known as backbenchers. The elected members of all other parties are in the opposition.

Their roles are to try to improve or defeat laws proposed by the party in power, and to speak out on behalf of the residents in their constituencies and the people across Canada who voted for their party.

Two political parties, the Liberals and the Conservatives, have dominated federal politics. However, from time to time, the number of political parties in Canada has grown to reflect the changing values of our diverse population. "Third parties" representing farmers and labour sprang up after World War I (the federal Progressives and provincial United Farmers parties) and in the 1930s (the CCF, now NDP, and Social Credit) because it was felt by many Canadians that the two established parties no longer represented their interests. Over the past decades, new regional parties have emerged to represent Quebec (the provincial Parti Québecois and federal Bloc Québecois) and Western Canadian interests (Reform/Canadian Alliance).

Finally, for a country to be democratic, it must protect the rights of its citizens by applying the rule of law. On three different occasions, groups who were perceived as a threat to public security lost those rights through the imposition of the War Measures Act. During World War I, the federal government stripped Ukrainian and Italian immigrants of their rights, labelled them "enemy aliens," interned many, and deported others. After the Japanese attack on Pearl Harbor in 1941, many Japanese-Canadian citizens living in British Columbia were declared "enemy aliens" and relocated to areas in the interior of BC, Alberta, Ontario, and Quebec. Then, during the October Crisis in Quebec in 1970, the federal government used the War Measures Act to suspend the civil liberties of Quebecers believed to be sympathetic to separatism.

Protection of civil liberties started slowly with the passing of ordinary statutes that set out a limited range of rights to which citizens were entitled. In 1960, Parliament passed the Bill of Rights, but it had no formal authority over any other laws.

The evolution of rights has varied from province to province. In most instances, it was spurred on by enlightened politicians or concerned citizens such as the suffragettes and the members of the Canadian Civil Liberties Association. The first comprehensive provincial Human Rights Code was passed by the Ontario government in 1962.

The BNA Act made no provisions for its own amendment. As an act of the British Parliament, it could be changed only by the British Parliament, but there were no rules about how these changes were to be agreed upon in Canada before being passed to London. Over time, more and more Canadians expressed a desire for constitutional sovereignty. In other words, they wanted to see the Constitution "patriated," that is, brought home to Canada so that it could be amended here according to clearly stated rules.

The first step in this lengthy process occurred in 1927. However, success was not realized until 1982, mostly because the federal and provincial governments could not agree on the rules for amending the patriated Constitution. After over 50 years of negotiation, the federal Parliament and nine of ten provincial legislatures finally agreed on a process of amendment and approved the Constitution Act of 1982. The last vestige of British involvement in Canadian political affairs occurred when the British Parliament passed the Canada Act. This officially ended British authority over their former colony by formally repealing the BNA Act and endorsing the Constitution Act.

One essential change in the new Constitution is the entrenchment of the Canadian Charter of Rights and Freedoms which defines and protects the fundamental civil, legal, and democratic rights of all Canadians. While it drew on rights that already existed in unwritten customs and traditions, and in the 1960 Bill of Rights, the Charter changed the relations between citizens and government by providing clear statements of rights and giving people the authority to defend those freedoms in court if necessary.

As we embark upon the 21st century, there will continue to be a myriad of issues to deal with. For democracy to be effective, Canadians must be willing to take an active role in public life by exercising the democratic power provided by our Constitution. We have an obligation to be involved, whether we act as individuals by voting or by writing letters of concern to an elected politician, or as a part of groups that either advocate policies we want implemented, or protest policies we oppose.

Rick Homan

THE OATH OF CITIZENSHIP

I swear (or affirm) that I will be faithful and bear true allegiance to Her Majesty Queen Elizabeth of Canada, Her Heirs and Successors, and that I will faithfully observe the laws of Canada and fulfill my duties as a Canadian citizen.

1860 - 1869

1864 — Sept: Charlottetown Conference

1864 — Oct: Quebec Conference

THE STRUGGLE FOR CONFEDERATION was not an easy one; nor did it happen as quickly as many had hoped. Internal and external forces were behind the struggle both for and against the scheme to bring the British North American colonies together.

Internally, intense rivalries between leading colonial politicians made Confederation seem inconceivable. Yet, the growing fear of assimilation among many French Canadians fuelled their search for better protection of their language and culture than that which the deadlocked political situation in the United Canadas could possibly provide.

In the late 1840s, external forces hastened Confederation as Great Britain shifted more responsibility to the colonies and repealed the Corn Laws in 1846, forcing the colonies to look elsewhere for markets. At the same time, a number of influential Americans claimed it was their "Manifest Destiny" to control the whole continent. The end of the Civil War left the U.S. with a huge army that many Americans felt should be turned against Britain because of her support for the South. The threat of invasion from the United States was made real when a group of Irish nationalists named Fenians conducted a series of raids between 1866 and 1871 in order to force Britain to leave Ireland.

As a result, both the British government and many colonists began to see that a federal union was necessary. Conferences were held in Charlottetown in September 1864, in Quebec City a month later, and in London in December 1866 to hammer out the final details for union.

In March 1867, the British Parliament passed the British North America Act that created the Dominion of Canada as a confederation with a strong central government and four small colonies governed within the British parliamentary system.

On 1 July 1867, Canada was formally born, with John A. Macdonald as the first Prime Minister. Within a few years, Canada more than quadrupled its size with the purchase of a huge tract of land in the Northwest from the Hudson Bay Company, and by convincing British Columbia to join the confederation. By 1871, Canada had become a country "from sea to sea to sea."

However, the Canada of 1869 was clearly a British nation with a substantial French fact. Little attention was paid to Native Canadians. Neither they nor the Métis were included in the negotiations to buy Rupert's Land, an oversight that was to lead directly to rebellion and the creation of the province of Manitoba.

ROAD TO CONFEDERATION

Voices of Support

(NAC C 10144)

John A. Macdonald *Conservative, Canada West:*

"…[T]he union of the colonies of British America, under one sovereign, is a fixed fact… If we can…obtain…a vigorous general government — we shall not be New Brunswickers, nor Nova Scotians, nor Canadians, but British Americans, under the sway of the British Sovereign… In the [Charlottetown] conference we have had no sectional prejudices or selfishness exhibited… — we all approached the subject feeling its importance; feeling that in our hands were the destinies of a nation …"

— Halifax, after Charlottetown Conference, 12 September 1864

Sir George Étienne Cartier, *leader of the French-speaking Parti Bleu in Canada East:*

"…Halifax through the intercolonial railroad will be the recipient of trade which now benefits Portland, Boston, and New York… it is as evident as the sun shines at noon that when the intercolonial railway is built — and it must necessarily be built if that confederation takes place — the consequence will be steamers almost daily leaving and arriving at … Halifax …"

— Halifax, after Charlottetown Conference, 12 September 1864

THE CONFEDERATION DEBATES

John A. Macdonald:

"…We had election after election – with the same result. Parties were so equally balanced, that the vote of one member might decide the fate of the Administration, and the course of legislation for a year or a series of years…None were more impressed by…the grave apprehensions that existed of a state of anarchy destroying our credit, destroying our prosperity, destroying our progress, than were the members of this present House; and the leading statesmen on both sides seemed to have come to the common conclusion, that some step must be taken to relieve the country from the deadlock…"

— Confederation Debates, 6 February 1865

Alexander Galt (represented the English minority in Canada East):

"…[H]ostile tariffs have interfered with the free interchange of the products of the labour of all the colonies, and one of the greatest and most immediate benefits to be derived from their union, will spring from the breaking down of these barriers and the opening up of the markets of all the provinces to the different industries of each… If we have reason to fear that one door [reciprocity with the U.S.] is about to be closed to our trade, it is the duty of the House to endeavour to open another…to seek by free trade with our fellow-colonists for a continued and uninterrupted commerce which will not be liable to be disturbed at the capricious will of any foreign country…"

— Confederation Debates, 7 February 1865

1866
Dec: The London Conference drafts legislation to create Canada

1866
Fenian Raids along Maine/New Brunswick border

1866
The British American Bank Note Company formed

1860–1869

George Brown, leader of the Clear Grits in Canada West: "…[T]his union will inspire new confidence in our stability, and exercise the most beneficial influence on all our affairs. I believe it will raise the value of our public securities, that it will draw capital to our shores, and secure the prosecution of all legitimate enterprise…"

— Confederation Debates, 8 February 1865

Thomas D'Arcy McGee, represented Irish Catholics in Canada East: "…They [the United States] coveted Florida, and seized it; they coveted Louisiana, and purchased it; they coveted Texas and stole it; and then they picked a quarrel with Mexico, which ended by their getting California…had we not the strong arm of England over us, we would not now have had a separate existence…"

— Confederation Debates, 9 February 1865

CONFEDERATION!
THE MUCH-FATHERED YOUNGSTER.

Pro-Confederation View of the Little Englanders

"The Little Englanders" were people in England who argued that the British North American colonies were a financial burden.

"I think it is natural and reasonable to hope that there is in the North American provinces a very strong attachment to Britain. But if they are to be constantly applying to us for guarantees for railways, and for grants for fortresses, and for works of defense, then I think it would be far better for them and us — cheaper for us — that they should become independent…"

— John Bright

Voices of Opposition

Antoine A. Dorion, *leader of the Parti Rouge in Canada East:*

"…I am opposed to this Confederation in which the militia, the appointment of the judges, the administration of justice and our most important civil rights, will be under the control of a General Government the majority of which will be hostile to Lower Canada, of a General Government invested with the most ample powers, whilst the powers of the local governments will be restricted, first, by the *Veto* reserved to the central authority, and further, by the concurrent jurisdiction of the general authority or government…"

— 6 March 1865

The Botheration Scheme

If we were to choose between the two systems, we would say at once, give us back the old Council of Twelve, with Downing Street behind it, rather than the exercise by a little knot of politicians 800 miles away of powers which could not fail to be grossly abused, and for the abuse of which it would be impossible to obtain redress.

—Joseph Howe, *Morning Chronicle* (Halifax) 11 January

*Men, hurrah for our own native isle, Newfoundland,
Not a stranger shall hold one inch of her strand;
Her face turns to Britain, her back to the Gulf,
Come near at your peril, Canadian Wolf.*

— Anti-Confederation song

Joseph Howe, Nova Scotia politician and journalist, led the movement against confederation

1866	1867	1868
Pro-Confederation party returned to power in New Brunswick	1 July: Confederation — John A. Macdonald becomes Canada's first Prime Minister	7 April: Canada's first political assassination — D'Arcy McGee

THE LONDON CONFERENCE

The London Conference, held at the Westminster Palace Hotel between December 1866 and March 1867, adopted the 72 (or Quebec) Resolutions drafted at the Quebec Conference of 1864. Little was changed, although Britain insisted that the name of the united colonies be Dominion of Canada rather than Kingdom of Canada. The London Resolutions then became the basis of the British North America Act (BNA). On the social scene, the major event appears to have been the marriage of John A. Macdonald and Agnes Bernard.

Choosing "Canada" as the new country's name was relatively easy, as was the choice of "Ontario" and "Quebec" for the two halves of the Province of Canada. However, difficulties arose in choosing a designation. The delegates wished it to be a kingdom; the British feared that such a title would anger the United States, and denied the request. An alternative, "Dominion" was suggested by Samuel Leonard Tilley, from a line in Psalm 72 of the Bible: "He shall have dominion also from sea to sea, and from the river unto the ends of the earth."

— Hector Langevin, letter to his brother in Quebec City

RIGHT TO VOTE IN CANADA

1867: Only men who own property allowed to vote

1878: Secret ballot used for first time in Canadian history

(Canadian Heritage Gallery ID #20029/J.D. Kelly, NAC C 6799)

"In framing the Constitution, care should be taken to avoid the mistakes and weaknesses of the United States system. Their primary error was reserving for the states all powers not given to the central government. We must reverse this… A strong central government is essential to the success of the experiment we are trying."

— J. A. Macdonald, 1864

▶ Great Seal of Canada. The engraving of the first Great Seal took two years to complete. The seal is used to mark important documents; a new seal is created for each new monarch.

THE BRITISH NORTH AMERICA ACT

FEDERAL SYSTEM WITH EXCERPT FROM BNA ACT, 1867
POWERS ASSIGNED EXCLUSIVELY TO THE FEDERAL GOVERNMENT

VI. Distribution of Legislative Powers
Powers of the Parliament

(1) The Public Debt and Property
(2) The Regulation of Trade and Commerce
(3) The Raising of Money by any Mode or System of Taxation
(5) Postal Service
(7) Militia, Military and Naval Service, and Defence
(12) Sea Coast and Inland Fisheries
(14) Currency and Coinage
(24) Indians, and Lands reserved for the Indians
(25) Naturalization and Aliens
(26) Marriage and Divorce
(27) The Criminal Law, except the Constitution of Courts of Criminal Jurisdiction, but including the Procedure in Criminal Matters

Exclusive Powers of Provincial Legislatures

92. In each Province the Legislature may exclusively make Laws in relation to Matters coming within the Classes of Subjects next hereinafter enumerated…
(2) Direct Taxation within the Province…
(7) The Establishment, Maintenance, and Management of Hospitals, Asylums, Charities…
(9) Shop, Saloon, Tavern, Auctioneer, and other Licences…
(12) The Solemnization of Marriage in the Province
(13) Property and Civil Rights in the Province

Education

93. In and for each Province the Legislature may exclusively make Laws in relation to Education, subject and according to the following Provisions:…

▲ The British North America Act (BNA), Constitution of the Dominion of Canada, was passed by the British Parliament in March 1867, and was proclaimed on 1 July 1867 (Dominion Day). It brought about the Confederation of the British colonies of Nova Scotia, New Brunswick, and the United Province of Canada (Upper and Lower Canada). The new Dominion remained a colony with no control over foreign affairs, although it was virtually self-governing in internal matters and trade policy. Provisions were made to protect the rights of denominational schools and to grant rights to Roman Catholic schools in Upper Canada and Protestant schools in Lower Canada.

1869	1869	1869
T. Eaton Company formed	22 June: Rupert's Land Act	Red River Rebellion

CONFEDERATION, 1 JULY 1867

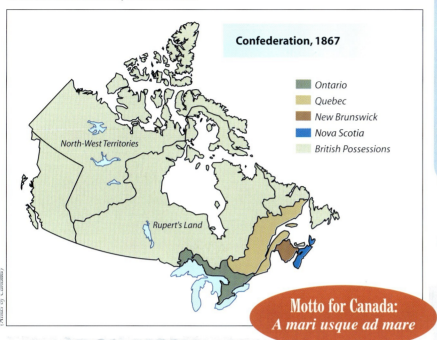

Motto for Canada: *A mari usque ad mare*

THE NATION'S BIRTHDAY!

*Let our voices be heard on this glorious morn
In anthems of joy for a NATION is born;
A companion for her who rules o'er the wave –
The foe of the tyrant – the friend of the slave….*

*Yes, our Nation is born on the bosom of Peace;
May her glory grow bright and her power increase;
O'er her head may no cloud of adversity rise,
But smooth be her pathway and stormless her skies.*

— Excerpt, *The Saint John Morning News*, 1 July 1867

"With the dawn of this summer morning, we hail the birthday of a new nation. A united British North America [Canada] takes its place among the nations of the world."

— George Brown

"Confederation Day!"

…So far as the people of Upper Canada are concerned, the inauguration of the new Constitution may well have been heartily rejoiced over as the brightest day in their calendar. — *The Globe*, 1 July 1867

The 1st of July

…Should some old pamphlet or bundle of newspapers of the present day find its way into some old chest, packed away and forgotten in some cellar or attic, should its resurrection two or three hundred years hence disclose the truth that there were actually people, in 1867, who poured out their wretched tirades against this Union; and talked of it as selling the rights and liberties of Nova Scotia, they could scarcely believe their eyes. It is difficult to realize it even now. Why do we seek Confederation?… because I wish to remain a loyal subject of Queen Victoria; because it will cement more closely these Colonies and the Mother Country; because England desired it in order to consolidate our strength; because it will ensure us against aggression…because it will promote the construction of our great public works, and in the end bring the commerce of the East across this American Continent; because it will give increased prosperity to every trade and occupation, and secure for our children…

—*Pictou Colonial Standard* (Nova Scotia) 2 July 1867

A Citizen's Voice

Monday last, 1st July, was the birthday of the Canadian Dominion. It was proclaimed as a public holiday and to some extent was observed in this town as such, but by no means as a day of rejoicing. Throughout the day, numerous flags were displayed half-mast, some of them draped in mourning… In several localities the men wore black weeds on their hats… An effigy of Dr. Tupper was suspended by the neck all afternoon on the spot known as The Devil's Half Acre and in the evening was burnt side by side with a live rat…

— Letter, unknown author from Yarmouth, NS, published in the *Yarmouth Herald*, 4 July 1867

RUPERT'S LAND

Rupert's Land Act, 1869
Assented to 22 June 1869

… Her Majesty the Queen may, pursuant to "The British North American Act, 1867," be pleased to admit Rupert's Land and the North-Western Territory into the Union or Dominion of Canada, before the next Session of the Canadian Parliament:…it is expedient to prepare for the transfer of the said Territories from the Local Authorities to the Government of Canada… and to make some temporary provision for the Civil Government of such Territories until more permanent arrangements can be made…

INSURRECTION OF THE FRENCH HALF BREEDS
The Road in Possession of the Rebels

What we have so long expected has at last taken place. Ever since the commencement of the last negotiations for the transfer of this Territory to the Dominion of Canada, a few individuals, who no doubt glory in their disloyalty to the Queen and their hatred of the Dominion…have been exceedingly busy in their efforts to create a spirit of opposition to the proposed transfer…

—*The Nor'wester and Pioneer* (Winnipeg) 26 October 1869

▲ Canada's annexation of Rupert's Land led to the uprising of the Métis under their leader, Louis Riel, in the Red River area. On 23 November 1869, Riel proposed a provisional government for the colony; in late December he became its president.

1870 - 1899

1870 — May: Manitoba Act passed

1871 — 16 May: British Columbia joins Confederation

1873 — 23 May: Prince Edward Island joins Confederation

HASTENED BY U.S. WESTERN EXPANSION and fear of American Manifest Destiny, Manitoba, British Columbia, and Prince Edward Island joined Canada in the years following Confederation, and the vast "empty" Northwest was divided into several territories administered by Ottawa.

The purchase of Rupert's Land in 1869 led to the Red River Rebellion and the establishment of the province of Manitoba a year later. In 1873, the Northwest Mounted Police was created to control the whiskey trade, to protect Native populations and settlers, and to patrol the West. Macdonald's first attempt to create a company to build the transcontinental railway led to the Pacific Scandal during which he and other Conservatives were accused of accepting bribes. The scandal led to the election of the first Liberal government in 1874 and the passing of the first Indian Act in 1876 to administer treaties and protect First Nations rights.

A number of important issues faced Canada in the 1880s. The Department of Indian Affairs was created to improve supervision of Native band councils; the Canadian Pacific Railway was provided with land, money, and tax exemptions in order to complete the transcontinental railroad by 1885; and the Ontario/Manitoba Boundary Dispute was settled in favour of Ontario.

In 1885, Louis Riel and the Métis confronted the federal government again. After the Red River Rebellion, many Métis had resettled along the Saskatchewan River. As the railway approached, the Métis and a number of First Nations, fearing the loss of their land and cultures, attacked. Riel was captured, tried, found guilty of treason, and executed. This controversial event was a catalyst for ongoing division between French and English Canadians. This rift widened in 1890 when an English Protestant government in Manitoba refused to fund French or Catholic schools as promised in the Manitoba Act of 1870. The split flared up again in 1899 when Laurier's decision to send troops (but not pay for them) to support the British in the Boer War upset both sides.

The secret ballot was introduced for the first time in the 1878 federal election, though women, Natives, and Asians were denied the vote; and property ownership remained a requirement to vote. Canada's initial First Ministers Conference was held in 1887 to promote a stronger relationship between the federal and provincial governments. Then, with the election of Wilfrid Laurier in 1896, Canada took its first, tentative steps toward multiculturalism. Clifford Sifton, the Minister of the Interior, reached out beyond Great Britain and the United States to encourage settlers from all over Europe, especially Eastern Europe, to fill the West.

RED RIVER REBELLION

(Saskatchewan Archives R-B 3809)

Execution of Thomas Scott

This morning the news spread that Thos. Scott one of the prisoners was condemned to be shot to-day… At about twelve O'Clock a.m. a large crowd gathered around the side door leading into Fort Garry. Scott was then brought out — it is said he prayed as he walked — a bandage was then put over his eyes and he knelt…

— Alexander Begg, 1 March 1870

▲ For the English speaking citizens of Ontario, the execution of Thomas Scott after a "farcical trial" was a symbol of Métis hostility. For Louis Riel, it meant exile to the United States.

TO THE LOYAL INHABITANTS OF MANITOBA

Her Majesty's Government, having determined upon stationing some troops amongst you, I have been instructed by the Lieut. General Commanding in the British North America to proceed to Fort Garry with the force under my Command.

Our mission is one of peace, and the sole object of the expedition is to secure Her Majesty's sovereign authority.

Courts of Law, such as are common to every portion of Her Majesty's Empire, will be duly established, and Justice will be impartially administered to all races and to all classes. The Loyal Indians or Half-Breeds being as dear to our Queen as any others of Her Loyal Subjects.

[sgd.] Colonel G.J. Wolseley, Commanding Red River Force.

— *New Nation Office*, 21 July 1870

THE DOMINION GROWS

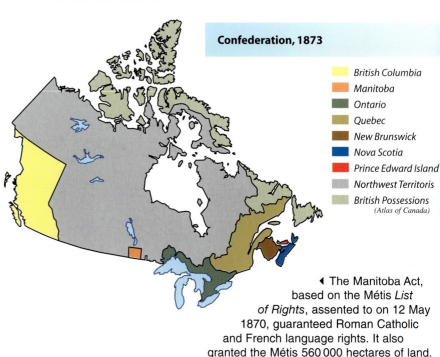

Confederation, 1873
- British Columbia
- Manitoba
- Ontario
- Quebec
- New Brunswick
- Nova Scotia
- Prince Edward Island
- Northwest Territoris
- British Possessions

(Atlas of Canada)

◀ The Manitoba Act, based on the Métis *List of Rights*, assented to on 12 May 1870, guaranteed Roman Catholic and French language rights. It also granted the Métis 560 000 hectares of land.

1875	1875	1878	1880
8 April: Northwest Territories Act passed	8 April: Supreme and Exchequer Court Act	John A. Macdonald elected; National Policy introduced	Sir Alexander Galt appointed first High Commissioner

1870–1899

British Columbia and Prince Edward Island

"…Apart from its being the policy of the British Government to unite all the British American Colonies in one great Federation, if we persist in remaining alone we shall be told by the Imperial Government that we are not fit for liberal institutions, and not prepared for self-government…

There is no difficulty in showing that Confederation will be beneficial to British Columbia; that is to say, Confederation on proper terms…. The public works proposed would make the population of the colony double what it is now…the construction of the railway alone would bring a very great increase to our labouring and productive population.…"

—The Hon. Mr. Robinson in the Legislative Council of British Columbia, 9 March 1870

▲ British Columbia joined Canada on 16 May 1871. The federal government agreed to take over BC's debts and promised to build a railway to connect BC with the rest of Canada.

Prince Edward Island's Proposed Entry Into Confederation

…*Governor Robinson of Prince Edward Island has written privately, and as if off his bat, to Lord Dufferin, saying that he thought that he could bring round his Government to consider the subject of Union, if Canada were still inclined in that direction.… Since then, Robinson telegraphed in cypher to know whether he was to understand that the island railway debt would be taken into consideration. The answer was, that the railway debt was a proper subject for negotiations.…*

—Sir John A. Macdonald in a letter to Sir John Rose, 13 December 1872

▲ Prince Edward Island joined Canada on 23 May 1873 with a federal promise to take over its debts and $800 000 to help buy back land from absentee British landowners.

PACIFIC SCANDAL

▲ In the House of Commons, April 1873, the Conservative Government was accused of accepting $325 000 in campaign funds from Sir Hugh Allan, after his company had been granted the contract to build the railway to the Pacific. The Pacific Scandal was the main issue in the election of 1874, which the Liberals under Alexander Mackenzie won in a decisive victory. The building of the railway would be delayed under the Liberals.

THE NATIONAL POLICY

"I move…that this House is of the opinion that the welfare of Canada requires the adoption of a National Policy, which, by a judacious readjustment of the Tariff, will benefit and foster the agricultural, the mining, the manufacturing and other interests of the Dominion; that such a policy will retain in Canada thousands of our fellow countrymen now obliged to expatriate themselves in search of the employment denied them at home, will restore prosperity to our struggling industries, now so sadly depressed, will prevent Canada from being made a sacrifice market, will encourage and develop an active interprovincial trade…"

—J.A. Macdonald introduced the Conservative Party's National Policy, 7 March 1878

▶ The National Policy was initiated by PM Macdonald in 1878 with the introduction of protective tariff policies to settle the West and complete the trans-continental railway. The National Policy tariff raised existing overall tariff rates from approximately 20% to 40% to shield Canadian manufacturers from foreigners, mostly American.

RIGHT TO VOTE IN CANADA

1880-1890: Thousands of people hold meetings, organize rallies, sign petitions, and donate money to gain the franchise for Canadian women

1880	1881	1882-84	1885	1885
Department of Indian Affairs created	Pacific Railway Act	Ontario/Manitoba Boundary Dispute	Land reserved for Mennonites in Manitoba	Nov: CPR completed

NORTH WEST MOUNTED POLICE

"Little as Canada might like it she has got to stable her elephant."
— Manitoba's Lt.-Gov. Alexander Morris on rowdy American whiskey traders in the Canadian West, 1872

- The North West Mounted Police was created in 1873. It was a small force of mounted riflemen with police and magistrate powers to enforce federal law in the North-West Territories. Their motto: *Maintien le Droit* (Maintain the Right).

- Sub-Inspector John French is flanked by colleagues in this 1874 photograph, the earliest known to have been taken of the force. French was later killed in a battle with Métis riflemen.

THE INDIAN ACT OF 1876

▲ Crowfoot, chief of the Blackfoot Confederacy, cradles an eagle's wing, symbol of his office. He ceded 50,000 square miles of fertile land in Mounties' Treaty No. 7. He did not join the North-West Rebellion in 1885 because he believed that the Métis and Indians had little chance to win.

"…If the Police had not come to the country, where would we be now? Bad men and whiskey were killing us so fast that very few, indeed, of us would have been left today. I wish them all good and trust that all our hearts will increase in goodness from this time forward. I am satisfied. I will sign the treaty."
— Crowfoot, 21 September 1876, on signing Treaty No. 7

INDIAN ACT, 1876

Reserves

5. The Superintendent-General may authorize surveys, plans and reports to be made of any reserve for Indians, shewing and distinguishing the improved lands, the forests and lands fit for settlement…
6. In a reserve, or portion of a reserve, subdivided by survey into lots, no Indian shall be deemed to be lawfully in possession of one or more of such lots, or part of a lot, unless he or she has been or shall be located for the same by the band, with the approval of the Superintendent-General:…

Surrenders

25. No reserve or portion of a reserve shall be sold, alienated or leased until it has been released or surrendered to the Crown for the purposes of this Act.

RIGHT TO VOTE IN CANADA

1885: The Electoral Franchise Act defines a "person" as a male. All people of Asian descent are excluded

"No Chinaman, Japanese or Indian shall have his name placed on the Register of Voters for any Electoral District, or be entitled to vote in any election."

— Provincial Elections Act of B.C., 1895

▸ Indian Treaty medals were a part of the regalia of the treaty ceremony. They offered a lasting reminder to all the participants of their treaty commitments. In 1873, several copies of a silver medal were ordered from England, at a cost of $24 each. They featured a bust of Queen Victoria and the inscription, "VICTORIA REGINA;" and on the reverse side, an Indian leader in war costume and a British officer shaking hands. The inscription of the reverse side reads: "INDIAN TREATY No…." The spaces were deliberately left blank and would be inscribed with the treaty number and date later.

1887	1896	1898	1899
Quebec City hosts First Ministers' Conference	Wilfrid Laurier becomes first French Canadian Prime Minister	Yukon becomes territory of Canada	Laurier commits Canadian troops and resources to Boer War

1870–1899

LOUIS RIEL AND THE NORTHWEST REBELLION

…"I believed for years I had a mission… If you take the plea of the defence that I am not responsible for my acts, acquit me completely, since I have been quarrelling with an insane and irresponsible Government….

…Although…I worked to better the condition of the people of Saskatchewan at the risk of my life, to better the condition of the people of the North-West, I have never had any pay. It has always been my hope to have a fair living one day."

— Louis Riel at his trial, 1885

"It is now my painful duty to pass the sentence of the court upon you…you shall be taken now from here to the police guard-room at Regina jail…and that on the 18th of September you be taken to the place appointed for your execution, and there be hanged by the neck till you are dead, and may God have mercy on your soul."

— Mr. Justice Richardson, trial judge, to Louis Riel, 1885

▲ Rebel leaders in the Armed Rising of 1885, in the North-West Territories of Canada. Left to right: Beardy, Big Bear, Louis Riel, White Cap, and Gabriel Dumont.

(Octave-Henri Julien, The Illustrated War News 1885)

END OF THE MACDONALD ERA

▲ Campaign poster of John A. Macdonald, 1891. In his final election campaign, Macdonald accused the Liberals, who were campaigning on a policy of free trade with the U.S., of "a deliberate conspiracy, by force, by fraud, or by both, to force Canada into the American Union…" Macdonald won the election, but fell ill soon after and passed away on 6 June.

(NAC C 6536)

"A British subject I was born, a British subject I will die."

— John A. Macdonald, 1891

"When this man is gone who will be there to take his place? Who else is there who knows the sheep or whose voice the sheep know?"

— Goldwin Smith, 1891

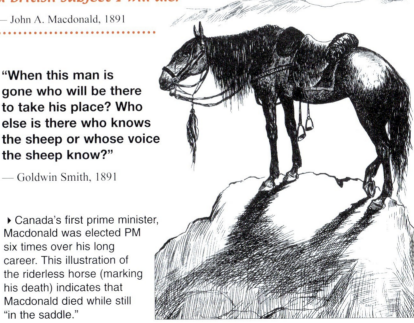

▶ Canada's first prime minister, Macdonald was elected PM six times over his long career. This illustration of the riderless horse (marking his death) indicates that Macdonald died while still "in the saddle."

1880-99: Four federal elections held

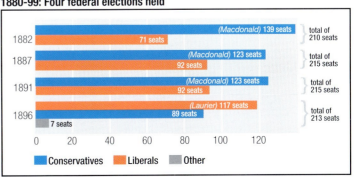

- 1882: (Macdonald) 139 seats; 71 seats — total of 210 seats
- 1887: (Macdonald) 123 seats; 92 seats — total of 215 seats
- 1891: (Macdonald) 123 seats; 92 seats — total of 215 seats
- 1896: (Laurier) 117 seats; 89 seats; 7 seats — total of 213 seats

■ Conservatives ■ Liberals ■ Other

1900 - 1919

1905 — 1 Sept: Alberta and Saskatchewan join Canada

1908 — Municipal Elections Act regulates voting on racial terms

THE CANADIAN ECONOMY BOOMED during the first decade of the 20th century. Federal and provincial governments promoted immigration, especially in the West, supported the building of new railways, spurred the development of resource-based industries, and created the provinces of Alberta and Saskatchewan. However, not everyone was able to profit from the good times. Chinese immigrants who had been brought to build the railroads were hit with a "head tax" that grew from $50 to $500, when the railroads were completed.

The Alaska Boundary Dispute of 1903 increased tensions between Canada and both Great Britain and the U.S. This led to the creation of the Department of External Affairs in 1910 that gave Canada more responsibility for diplomatic relations. Policies designed to weaken Canadian-British ties, especially Reciprocity with the United States and the Naval Service Bill, angered British Canadians and were significant in the 1911 defeat of the Liberals by Borden's Conservatives.

The outbreak of World War I set civil rights further back. Hundreds of Ukrainian, Italian, and other Eastern European immigrants were labelled as "enemy aliens" and interned in camps under the 1914 War Measures Act.

Political rights for others, however, were strengthened during the war. Due to the efforts of suffragists such as Nellie McClung, women became eligible to vote provincially, first in Manitoba in 1916, then in five other provinces, and federally by the end of the war. In 1915, Elections Canada made it compulsory that employees be given time off on Election Day to vote.

As the war dragged on, personal income tax and Victory Bonds were introduced to help cover the war debt. Then, in 1917, the Conscription issue split French and English Canadians. Borden called an election which he won, in part, by changing the election law to disqualify conscientious objectors, eliminate voting rights of citizens from Germany and Austria-Hungary, and give the vote to only women in the armed forces or whose male relatives were fighting overseas. He also created a Union Government of Liberals and Conservatives which supported conscription. This government passed the Women's Franchise Act of 1918 that granted all women the right to vote in federal elections.

By the end of the war, Canada had achieved greater world recognition, took a seat at the Paris Peace Conference, signed the Versailles Peace Treaty, and joined the League of Nations. At home, demands for major social and political change were heard. A working class wave of revolt culminated in the Winnipeg General Strike in 1919. As the strike was crushed and its leaders jailed, labour leaders turned to electoral politics.

(William James Topley/NAC C 1971)

> "...The one aim that I have is to unite all the races on this continent into a Canadian nation..."
> —Wilfrid Laurier, PM 1896-1911, address

MINORITY PERSPECTIVES

Raising The Head Tax On Immigrants: Another Brick In The Wall

Remember the head tax in the Chinese Immigration Act? Well, it obviously hasn't stemmed the tide of Asian immigration enough to please the legislators. The federal government decides to raise its tax on immigrants. The tax is raised to $500 in a time when most Chinese make less than a dollar a day…

— *Canadian Magazine*, 1900

Uncle John and Prescott have been using grandmother shamefully all summer….they have been trying to turn her out…Grandfather's absurd will put her completely in their power — the power of selfish, domineering men eaten up with greed. Grandmother told them she would not leave the home where she had lived and worked for sixty years…

—L.M. Montgomery, *Selected Journals*, Vol. 1 (1889-1910)

"My race remembers with most tender gratitude the generosity and kindness manifested on the part of the people of the Dominion of Canada in the dark days of slavery. I remember as a child hearing my parents and the older slaves speak of Canada with a tenderness and faith for what it would do for our race that I had no definite idea that it had any tangible, visible place. I thought it was an invisible ideal."

— American civil rights advocate, Booker T. Washington, in a 1906 Ottawa speech

**Go forth, nor bend to greed of white men's hands,
By right, by birth we Indians own these lands…**

— Pauline Johnson, "A Cry from an Indian wife," in *Flint and Feathers*, 1912

A Citizen's Voice

"…To many people in Canada this imperialism is a tainted word. It is too much associated with…subservience to English people and English ideas…. But there is and must be for the future of our country, a higher and more real imperialism than this…the imperialism of any decent citizen that demands for his country its proper place in the councils of the Empire and in the destiny of the world. In this sense, imperialism means but the realization of a greater Canada, the recognition of a wider citizenship.
 I…am an Imperialist because I will not be a Colonial…."

— Stephen Leacock, "Greater Canada: An Appeal," *University Magazine*, April 1907

1909	1910	1911
Department of External Affairs created — A. Galt chosen to represent Canada in London	Naval Service Bill proposed	Reciprocity with U.S. rejected

EXPANSION OF CONFEDERATION

EDMONTON HAD GALA DAY
City Did Itself Grand on the Occasion of the Inauguration Ceremonies of the West.

Edmonton, Sept. 1— The Formal inauguration of Alberta took place at 12 o'clock today. Before that the Mounted Police, to the number of 200, under Commissioner Perry gave a magnificent exhibition drill. They were marched past the Governor at a walk, trot, canter and gallop. They presented a fine appearance, and were cheered to the echo. …A salute of 21 guns then fired… Sir Wilfrid Laurier then addressed the people, and was well received…

It is estimated that 15,000 people are present. Sir Wilfrid addressed the French people in that language….

—*Daily Standard*, 2 September 1905

1900 – 1919

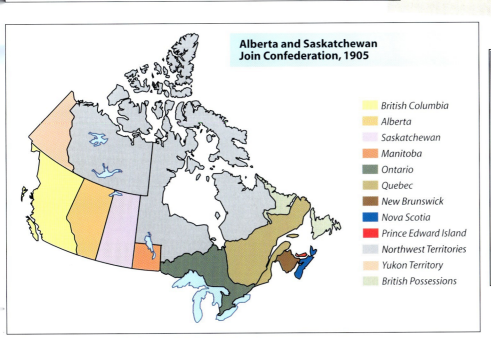

ALBERTA ACT
An Act to establish and provide for the Government of the Province of Alberta
[Assented to 20 July 1905]

2. The territory comprised within the following boundaries…is hereby established as a province of the Dominion of Canada, to be called and known as the province of Alberta….

3. *The provisions of the Constitution Acts, 1867 to 1886* shall apply to the province of Alberta in the same way and to the like extent as they apply to the provinces heretofore compromised in the Dominion…

▲ The Alberta Act was similar in wording to the Saskatchewan Act and both were enacted at the same time, in 1905.

RECIPROCITY

◄ In 1910-11, the Laurier government negotiated a Reciprocity Agreement with the U.S. that allowed a large number of trade items to pass back and forth across the Canada-U.S. border without duty. The agreement was rendered null and void when Laurier lost the 1911 election to the anti-Reciprocity Conservatives under Robert Borden. Not until 1989 was a Free Trade Agreement enacted.

Sir Wilfrid Laurier: *"This here Halifax platform feels like it was made of India rubber."*
R.L. Borden: *"Well, why not? Wasn't it made to bounce you?"*

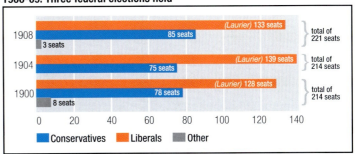

1900-09: Three federal elections held

Year	Conservatives	Liberals	Other	Total
1908	85 seats	(Laurier) 133 seats	3 seats	total of 221 seats
1904	75 seats	(Laurier) 139 seats		total of 214 seats
1900	78 seats	(Laurier) 128 seats	8 seats	total of 214 seats

1914	1914	1916	1917
War Measures Act created	Law passed giving workers time off during election to vote	Women in Manitoba, Saskatchewan, and Alberta become eligible to vote	Military Service Act passed

THE GREAT WAR

▲ In WW I, persons of "Enemy Alien" origin (that is, immigrants from countries with which Canada was at war) were subject to internment if reasonable grounds could be advanced that they might engage in espionage.

▼ To support the war effort, the government used a variety of approaches to raise money from institutional investors and the general public, such as Victory Bonds, War Savings Certificates, and War Savings Stamps.

WAR MEASURES ACT, 1914

3. The provisions of sections 6,10,11, and 13 of this Act shall only be in force during war, invasion, or insurrection, real or apprehended.
8. Any ship or vessel used or moved, or any…merchandise dealt with contrary to any order or regulation made under this Act, may be seized and detained…
13.…[T]he Governor in Council may from time to time authorize the appointment of such numbers of constables, supernumerary constables, scouts and boys…as he thinks necessary.

A Citizen's Voice

"We slept on the bare floor…we were treated in the same manners as prisoners of war… My thoughts were disturbing: 'What a commentary on a system that uses jails to drive fear into the hearts of innocent people and subjects them to forced labour.'"

—Philip Yanowsky, describing his WW I internment, in "Under Native and Alien Skies" in *Land of Pain, Land of Promise*, 1978

CONSCRIPTION

"My experiences in France have shown me, as a soldier, the necessity of conscription if we desire to maintain at full strength our fighting divisions to the end of the war."

— Arthur Currie, Commander of the Canadian Corps in France, 1917

"…[I]t is my duty to announce to the House that early proposals will be made to provide by compulsory military enlistment on a selective basis, such reinforcement as may be necessary to maintain the Canadian army in the field…"

— Prime Minister Borden, 11 June 1917

A Citizen's Voice

"In Sydney after the war started, quite a few Blacks volunteered for active service and were told point blank, 'We don't want you. This is a white man's war.' However, around 1917, the Canadian Army was up against it; they had lost a lot of men in France. At that point, they were willing to take anyone. Conscription came in, and then they took the Blacks and Whites. You had no choice — you had to go."

— Coloured veteran Isaac Phills of Dartmouth, quoted in *The Black Battalion 1916-1920, Canada's Best Kept Military Secret* by Calvin Ruck

1917	1918	1919	1919
Wartime Elections Act passed	Electoral Franchise Upon Women Act passed	Canada given seat at Paris Peace Conference	Canadian National Railway becomes Crown corporation

1900–1919

WOMEN: THE RIGHT TO VOTE

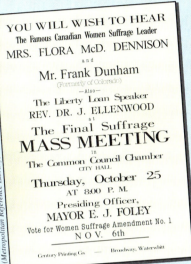

◀ Poster announcing a suffrage meeting.

"Don't be submissive. Don't be docile. Don't be ladylike. Don't dread being conspicuous. Now is the time for deeds not words. Remember you are fighting for liberty… Concentrate all your efforts on the Dominion Parliament…. Go to Mr. Borden in your thousands and demand votes for women at this Session — not at some long distant future, but now."

— Barbara Wylie, suffragette leader, Montreal, November 1912

▲ Suffragists of the Winnipeg Equality League pose with a stack of petitions for the franchise, 1915. The women in Manitoba were the first to win the right to vote in provincial elections in January 1916.

"I conceive that women are entitled to the franchise on their merits, and it is upon this basis that this Bill is presented to Parliament to its consideration. It is our belief that the influence of women exercised in this way will be good influence in public life. We believe that beneficial results have ensued wherever the franchise has been granted them."

— PM. Borden, moving second reading of Bill No. 3 giving franchise to women, House of Commons, 22 March 1918

"I say that the Holy Scriptures, theology, ancient philosophy, Christian philosophy, history, anatomy, physiology, political economy, and feminine psychology all seem to indicate that place of women in this world is not amid the strife of political arena but in her home…"

— Jean Joseph Dennis, opposing Bill No. 3, House of Commons, 11 April 1918

WOMEN GET FEDERAL VOTE

Ottawa, Ontario — Robert Laird Borden passes Canada Elections Act; gives all Canadian women over 21, the right to vote in federal elections only.

— *Manitoba Free Press,* 1918

INCOME WAR TAX

INCOME WAR TAX ACT, 1917

…The following incomes shall not be liable to taxation hereunder,
(a) the income of the Governor General of Canada…
(d) the income of any religious, charitable, agricultural and educational institutions, Boards of Trade and Chambers of Commerce…

◀ Sir Robert Laird Borden, Prime Minister of Canada from 1911-20, introduced income tax, nationalization of Canadian northern railway, Military Service Act (which led to Conscription Crisis 1917), and Military Voters Act; created Union Government 1917; attended Paris Peace Conference 1919, Washington Conference 1921, and League of Nations 1921.

RIGHT TO VOTE IN CANADA

1916: Women in Manitoba become the first women in Canada to win the right to vote in provincial elections

1917: The Wartime Election Act takes away the right to vote from Canadian citizens who were born in an enemy country and obtained citizenship after March 1902. Those whose first language or parents' language is the language of an enemy country also lose the right to vote
Wives, sisters and mothers of serviceman win the vote in federal elections. The right to vote is extended to Aboriginal Canadians in the armed forces

1918: All adult women win the right to vote in federal elections, except those of Asian, Inuit, or Status Indian Descent

1910-19: Two federal elections held

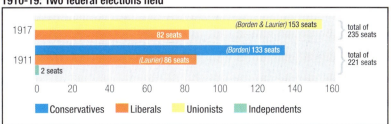

- 1917: (Borden & Laurier) 153 seats; 82 seats — total of 235 seats
- 1911: (Borden) 133 seats; (Laurier) 86 seats; 2 seats — total of 221 seats

Conservatives ■ Liberals ■ Unionists ■ Independents

1920 - 1929

1920 — National Progressive Party established

1920 — Col. Oliver Mowat appointed first Chief Electoral Officer

1921 — Agnes Macphail: first woman elected to House of Commons

Throughout Canada's first half a century, federal politics was dominated by two parties, the Liberals and the Conservatives. In the 1920s, this two-party system was replaced by a multi-party system. In the 1921 federal election, a new Western-based protest party, the Progressives, elected 64 MPs, 14 more than the third place Conservatives. Nevertheless, the Conservatives were declared the Official Opposition, a role normally played by the second-place party. Two years before that, a coalition of the United Farmers of Ontario and the Independent Labour Party won the first postwar election in Ontario. In 1921, the United Farmers of Alberta was elected and held power until 1935.

In 1921, Agnes Macphail was elected as the first woman MP in Ontario just three years after women gained the right to vote in federal elections. While the Elections Act had been changed to remove the right of provinces to determine who could vote in federal elections, First Nations people and many minorities such as Asians were still denied the right to vote.

In 1926, a political crisis threatened the very basis of Canada's constitutional monarchy. Mackenzie King's Liberals, with support from the Progressives, had held on to power despite losing the 1925 election to Arthur Meighen's Conservatives. When King lost a vote of non-confidence in 1926, he asked Governor General Byng to dissolve Parliament and call a new election. Byng refused and asked Meighen to form a government. When the Conservatives in turn lost a non-confidence motion, Byng had no choice but to call an election. The Progressives disappeared from the political scene, King won the election, and Byng was replaced as Governor General.

During this period of political upheaval, the first part of what would become Canada's "social safety net" was created. In 1927, King honoured a pledge he had made to J.S. Woodsworth in exchange for the support of the "Ginger Group" — Old Age Pensions, which guaranteed poor seniors $20 per month, was established.

However, politics in the 1920s was not entirely progressive. In 1928, the Alberta government passed a law forcing the inmates of provincial mental institutions to be sterilized. That same year, the Supreme Court of Canada ruled that women were not eligible for appointment to the Senate because they were not "persons" within the meaning of the Constitution, the BNA Act. A year later, the Judicial Committee of the British Privy Council overturned that decision, an event that is today celebrated as "Persons' Day" on 18 October.

THE KING-BYNG AFFAIR

Your Excellency having declined to accept my advice to place your signature to the Order-in-Council with reference to a dissolution of parliament...I hereby tender to Your Excellency my resignation as Prime Minister of Canada...

As a refusal by a Governor General to accept the advice of a Prime Minister is a serious step at any time...there will be raised, I fear, by the refusal on Your Excellency's part to accept the advice tendered a grave constitutional question without precedent in the history of Great Britain for a century, and in the history of Canada since Confederation...

— Letter from W.L. Mackenzie King to Governor General Byng, 28 June 1926

...You advise me "that as, in your opinion, Mr. Meighen is unable to govern the country, there should be another election with the present machinery to enable the people to decide." My contention is that Mr. Meighen has not been given a chance of trying to govern, or saying that he cannot do so, and that all reasonable expedients should be tried before resorting to another Election....

— Letter from Governor General Byng to W.L. Mackenzie King, 29 June 1926

As already telegraphed, Mr. Mackenzie King asked me to grant him dissolution. I refused. Thereupon he resigned and I asked Mr. Meighen to form a Government, which has been done. Now this constitutional or unconstitutional act of mine seems to resolve itself into these salient features. A Governor General has the absolute right of granting dissolution or refusing it. The refusal is a very dangerous decision, it embodies the rejection of the advice of the accredited Minister, which is the bed-rock of Constitutional Government...

...But I have to wait the verdict of history to prove my having adopted a wrong course and this I do with an easy conscience that, right or wrong, I have acted in the interests of Canada, and have implicated no one else in my decision.

— Letter from Governor General Byng to Mr. L. S. Amery, The Secretary of State for Dominion Affairs, 30 June 1926

▲ The King-Byng Affair, a conflict between PM King and Governor General Byng, led to a demand for clarification of the power of the Queen's Representative. The Balfour Report followed discussion of this and other inter-imperial relations.

THE BALFOUR REPORT
Signed 19 November 1926
Report of Inter-Imperial Relations Committee

...We refer to the group of self-governing communities composed of Great Britain and the Dominions. Their position and mutual relations may be readily defined. They are autonomous communities within the British Empire, equal in status, in no way subordinate one to another in any aspect of their domestic or external affairs, though united by a common allegiance to the Crown, and freely associated as members of the British Commonwealth of Nations....

1924	1925	1926	1927
26 Jan: Red Ensign unfurled as Canada's official flag	United Farmers Party, led by Henry Wise Wood, wins Alberta election	Vincent Massey becomes first Foreign Minister	Mar: Old Age Pensions Act assented

WOMEN: ANOTHER STEP FORWARD

"Homosexuals are no more responsible for their sexual preferences than we are."
— Agnes Macphail, 1921

◂ Feminist and anti-militarist Agnes Macphail was the first woman elected to the federal Parliament in 1921.

"The exclusion of women from all public offices is a relic of days more barbarous than ours."
— the Judicial Committee of the Privy Council, 1929

PERSON'S CASE, 1929

(5) ...their Lordships have come to the conclusion that the word 'persons' in s. 24 includes members both of the male and female sex, and that, therefore, the question propounded by the Governor General should be answered in the affirmative, and that women are eligible to be summoned to and become members of the Senate of Canada, and they will humbly advise His Majesty accordingly.

And it is because the finding of the Privy Council that we are "persons," once and for all, will do so much to merge us into the human family, that we are filled with gratitude and joy....

...[T]here had to be a ruling on it. Women have been regarded as creatures of relationships rather than human beings with direct responsibilities. That is why one senator said women could not sit in the Senate, and give unbiased judgements, that is, married women, because they would naturally have to do what their husbands wished them to do. He might have gone on, and said any woman who had a male relative would owe her first allegiance to him. The world has gone on since that law prevailed, but the dear old fellow hasn't noticed...

We cannot understand the mentality of men who dare to set the boundaries of women's work. We object to barriers, just as the range horses despise fences...we believe in equality.

— Nellie McClung, "A Retrospect," in *The Country Guide*, December 1929

The BNA set membership in the Senate to "persons." In 1928, the Canadian Supreme Court ruled that women were not persons. Activists fought this to the highest court of the British Empire, the Privy Council, and won, in October 1929, opening the doors of the Senate to women.

"...mock congratulations and ironic expressions of gratitude greeted the news from London that their lordships had decided that women were legally persons within the meaning of the B.N.A. Act and were consequently entitled to sit in the Senate."
— *Winnipeg Tribune*

In 1930, Cairine Reay Mackay Wilson was first female appointed to the Senate.

1920 – 1929

THE OLD AGE PENSIONS ACT
Assented to 31 March 1927

...8. (1) Provision shall be made for the payment of a pension to every person who, at the date of the proposed commencement of the pension:
(a) is a British subject, or, being a widow, who is not a British subject, was such before her marriage;
(b) has attained the age of seventy years;
(c) has resided in Canada for twenty years immediately preceding the date aforesaid;...
(e) is not an Indian defined by the Indian Act;
(f) is not in receipt of an income of as much as three hundred and sixty-five dollars ($365) a year;...

▴ Old Age Pensions, federal program agreed to by the Liberal government of PM King in 1926 to repay the Ginger Group for its support of the minority Liberal government over the preceding years.

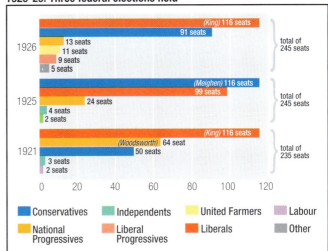

1920-29: Three federal elections held

1926: (King) 116 seats Liberals; 91 seats Conservatives; 13 seats National Progressives; 11 seats United Farmers; 9 seats Liberal Progressives; 5 seats Other — total of 245 seats

1925: (Meighen) 116 seats Conservatives; 99 seats Liberals; 24 seats National Progressives; 4 seats Liberal Progressives; 2 seats Independents — total of 245 seats

1921: (King) 116 seats Liberals; (Woodsworth) 64 seats National Progressives; 50 seats Conservatives; 3 seats Independents; 2 seats Labour — total of 235 seats

Legend: Conservatives, Independents, United Farmers, Labour, National Progressives, Liberal Progressives, Liberals, Other

1930 - 1939

1930
Cairine Reay Mackay Wilson becomes first woman appointed to Senate

1931
Statute of Westminster grants Canada full autonomy from Britain

THE "DIRTY THIRTIES" WAS a decade of economic devastation and political upheaval throughout the world. New political movements arose and old political ideas were thrown out as unworkable in the face of the Great Depression. The decade gave rise to three new national political parties — the Reconstruction Party, the Co-operative Commonwealth Federation (CCF), and Social Credit Party — and a new political force in Quebec, Maurice Duplessis' Union Nationale.

Three years after its founding in Calgary and the adoption of the Regina Manifesto in 1933, the CCF elected seven MPs, including its first leader, J.S. Woodsworth, in the 1935 federal election that returned Mackenzie King's Liberals to power. The right-wing Social Credit Party elected 17 MPs, mostly from Alberta. That same year, the Social Credit Party of Alberta, under the charismatic leadership of radio evangelist "Bible Bill" Aberhart, swept to victory in a provincial election that saw every member of the governing United Farmers party thrown out of office. The next year, a former Conservative, Maurice Duplessis, led his new, right-wing Union Nationale party to victory in Quebec. It looked as if the two-party system was gone forever.

To survive, the old-line parties were forced to change. In the United States, Franklin D. Roosevelt created a new Democratic Party coalition to defeat the Republicans in 1932, then quickly implemented a series of New Deal policies to get people working again. These measures were so popular on both sides of the border that Conservative PM R. B. Bennett announced his own "New Deal" in 1935. While Mackenzie King was initially reluctant to adopt these new approaches to government involvement in the economy, he did appoint the Royal Commission on Dominion-Provincial Relations (the Rowell-Sirois Commission) in 1937. In 1940, the commission recommended many new policy changes based on the ideas of British economist, John Maynard Keynes.

After decades of inching closer to full independence from Britain, Canada and other former British colonies were finally granted full legislative power over both internal and external affairs by the passage of the Statute of Westminster in 1931.

As the Depression decade drew to a close, war again loomed. King George VI and Queen Elizabeth triumphantly became the first reigning monarchs to tour Canada during that last summer of peace. Then, six days after Great Britain declared war on Nazi Germany and her allies, Canada entered the war.

THE GREAT DEPRESSION

▲ The Single Men's Unemployed Association parading in Toronto, circa 1930.

> **FEDERAL RELIEF CAMPS ORDER IN COUNCIL**
> **Proclaimed 8 October 1932**
>
> …That there are certain works that can be undertaken by the Department of National Defence…with advantage in the general interest of Canada, and also to provide an occupation for the single homeless men, who may thus be provided with accommodation, subsistence, and a cash allowance… That the works…are as follows:
> 1. Construction and development of a Trans Canada Airway
> 2. Repairs, renovations and renewals of certain portions of the Old Fortifications
> 3. Repairs, renovations and renewals of portions of the Citadel at Halifax, N.S.…

Out of Work

There is a street down-town, where all day long,
Go silent men with lagging feet that look
As they were more familiar with rough ways
Than greasy pavements and the crowded streets;
Grey men with lagging feet and mutinous mouths —
Oh, fear those mutinous mouths, those lagging feet,
Those unseen, unraised eyes that brood and brood
On living death.

— Annie Charlotte Dalton, 1929

> By 1933… the railway towns of the West were overrun in the summers by young transients, who dropped off freight trains to try to exchange a day's work in the garden for a square meal.
>
> — John Gray, *The Winter Years*

▲ The unemployed demonstrate during the Depression, October 1933.

	1932	1935	1933
	CCF (Co-operative Commonwealth Federation) established	Social Credit Party elected in Alberta	Regina Manifesto

Decline in average income per person, by province		
	1928-29	1933
Saskatchewan	$478	$135
Alberta	548	212
Manitoba	466	240
British Columbia	594	314
Prince Edward Island	278	154
Ontario	549	310
Quebec	391	220
New Brunswick	292	180
Nova Scotia	322	207
Canada	471	247

A Citizen's Voice

Dear Prime Minister R.B. Bennett,

It is with very humble heart I take the opportunity of writing this letter to you, to ask if you will please send for the underwear in the Eaton's order, made out and enclosed in this letter. My husband will be 64 in December and his neuritis is very bad. We have had very few crops for the last three years, not enough at all to pay taxes and live, and this year's crops are a complete failure. My husband is drawing wood on the wagon for 34 miles, it takes two days for a trip and he has to sleep out under the wagon. It is cold and windy. I am writing this in the hope that you will send for this underwear for him, as we have no money ourselves.... If only I can get this underwear for my husband, I can manage for myself...

— 28 September 1933

▲ Prime Minister R.B. Bennett was a very wealthy man who had never experienced poverty. During the early years of the Depression, Bennett was inundated with letters from destitute Canadians pleading for help.

LOOSENING THE TIES TO BRITAIN

BENNETT'S NEW DEAL

◀ PM R.B. Bennett's "New Deal," a reform platform modelled on that of U.S. President F.D. Roosevelt, was rejected by voters as "too little, too late."

"The time has come when I must speak to you with the utmost frankness about our national affairs.... In the last five years, great challenges have taken place in the world.... The world is in tragic circumstances. The signs of recovery are few and doubtful. The signs of trouble are many, and they do not lessen. The world is searching pathetically for safety and prosperity. it will find them only when each nation, resolute to effect its own regeneration, will come to a meeting place with all the others, in the spirit which declares that even the most powerful among them has no real economic independence of the rest.... The courage of our people, the robustness of our economic structure, the effectiveness of your government, are all overwhelmingly attested by the fact that, though in 1932 we were in a most critical condition, we did not perish. On the contrary, we fought back strongly. I pay my tribute of profound admiration to the gallantry and patience of the people of Canada in those terrible times."

— Prime Minister R.B. Bennett, radio address from Ottawa, January 1935

◀ Academic medal awarded to Mary A. MacDonald of Antigonish, Nova Scotia in 1935. The Governor General's Academic Medal was first awarded in 1873. It recognizes the value of an educated citizenry. Today it is awarded to the top student in a graduating class, from high school to post graduate degrees.

▼ The Statute of Westminster, 1931, an act of the British Parliament, gave Canada (and other Dominions) autonomy in external relations and independence in domestic policy. The statute effectively created the modern Commonwealth.

1930 – 1939

STATUTE OF WESTMINSTER
Assented to 11 December 1931

AN ACT TO GIVE EFFECT TO CERTAIN RESOLUTIONS PASSED BY IMPERIAL CONFERENCES HELD IN THE YEARS 1926 AND 1930

1. In this Act the expression "Dominion" means any of the following Dominions...the Dominion of Canada, the Commonwealth of Australia, the Dominion of New Zealand, the Union of South Africa, the Irish Free State and Newfoundland....

2. (2) No law and no provision of any law made after the commencement of this Act by the Parliament of a Dominion shall be void or inoperative on the ground that it is repugnant to the law of England, or to the provisions of any existing or future Act of Parliament of the United Kingdom...

3. ...(T)he Parliament of a Dominion has full power to make laws having extraterritorial operation.

4. No Act of Parliament of the United Kingdom...shall extend, or be deemed to extend, to a Dominion as part of the law of that Dominion, unless it is expressly declared in that Act that the Dominion has requested, and consented to the enactment thereof.

7. (1) Nothing in this Act shall be deemed to apply to the repeal, amendment or alteration of the British North America Acts, 1867 to 1930, or any order, rule, or regulation made thereunder.

1935	1936	1936	1937
PM Bennett introduces his party's "New Deal"	Union Nationale elected in Quebec	23 June: Canadian Broadcasting Act passed	Rowell-Sirois Commission set up

1935 ELECTION CAMPAIGN

"KING OR CHAOS"

▸ Prime Minister King, who had been elected in the 1920s by insisting on Canada's autonomy, is viewed here during the 1935 election campaign, the theme of which was "King or Chaos."

(PAC C132)

▸ 1935 election campaign poster.

VOTE LIBERAL BECAUSE—
1. You do not want a one-man government in Ottawa
2. You want your representatives to make a contribution to the Government in your interest
3. You want a People's Government
4. You do not want to elect more rubber stamps
5. You do not want the "the iron heel of ruthlessness" in Canada

VOTE LIBERAL
issued by the National Liberal Federation
114 Wellington St. Ottawa

◂ W.L. Mackenzie King driving the Bennett Buggy in Sturgeon Valley, Saskatchewan. During the Great Depression, the Bennett Buggy, a horse-drawn car with the motor removed, saved the owner the expense of buying gasoline.

THIRD PARTIES

▴ Maurice Duplessis *(left)* was premier of Quebec from 1936-39, and again in 1944 until his death 15 years later. He was an erratic, corrupt, effective manager and a lasting political presence.

THE UNION NATIONALE PLATFORM, 1934

IV. Economic reforms
   1. To break, by every means possible, the stranglehold which big business has upon the province and the municipalities....

VI. Political and Administrative Reforms
   1. Good management and honesty in the public administration;

VII. Electoral reforms
   2. Compulsory voting (measure subject to plebiscite);
   4. Identity cards in cities exceeding 10,000 souls;

VIII. Fiscal Reforms
   6. Redistribution of federal, provincial and municipal taxes in order that the commercial corporations and certain classes of individuals, who often enjoy exemptions or unjust assessments, may contribute to the public coffers in an equitable manner.

COOPERATIVE COMMONWEALTH FEDERATION PROGRAMME

The CCF is a federation of organizations whose purpose is the establishment in Canada of a co-operative Commonwealth in which the principle regulating production, distribution and exchange will be on the supplying of human needs and not the making of profits.

We aim to replace the present capitalist system, with its inherent injustice and inhumanity, by a social order from which the domination and exploitation of one class by another will be eliminated, in which economic planning will supersede unregulated private enterprise and competition, and in which genuine democratic self-government, based upon economic equality will be possible...

— Adopted at the First National Convention, Regina, Saskatchewan, July 1933

◂ The CCF was founded in 1932 when representatives from farm, labour, intellectual, and socialist groups assembled in the Calgary Labour Temple. J.S. Woodsworth *(above)* was its first leader.

1937	1939	1939	1939
Air Canada created	National Film Board established	10 Sept: Canada declares war on Germany	3 June: Official Secrets Act

THE SOCIAL CREDIT PLATFORM, 1935

1. Finance and the Distribution of Goods
(a) The Cessation of Borrowing from Outside Sources and the creation of our own Credit, thus gradually eliminating heavy interest charges and retaining our own purchasing power.
(b) The Distribution of Purchasing Power to bona fide citizens by the means of Basic Dividends sufficient to secure the necessities of food, clothing and shelter…
(c) The establishment of a Just Price on all goods and services and the regulation of the price spread on all goods and services sold or transferred within the bounds of the province…

▸ William Aberhart, Premier of Alberta and founder of the Social Credit League, addressing a rally in July 1937 in Calgary. The Social Credit advocated $25 dividends for all citizens.

WORLD WAR II

"It is what we prevent, rather than what we do that counts most in Government."
—Mackenzie King, 26 August 1936

"Hitler has said, 'Whoever lights the torch of war in Europe can wish for nothing but chaos.' 'Nothing but chaos;' that is what the leader of the Nazi party in Germany is seeking to bring upon the world today. And it is to prevent chaos becoming the fate of this and other lands that it becomes our duty, as citizens of Canada, to stand to a man in the defence of our country and at the side of Great Britain in the defence of freedom."
— PM Mackenzie King, House of Commons address, 1939

▲ W.L. Mackenzie King and members of the Cabinet broadcasting to the Canadian people following Great Britain's declaration of war, 3 September 1939. Left to right: C.G. Power, Ernest Lapointe, W.L. Mackenzie King, Norman Rogers.

◂ An excited crowd mills around a Montreal news stand on 3 September 1939, a week before Canada officially entered the war.

A PROCLAMATION

…Now therefore we do hereby declare and proclaim that a State of War with the German Reich exists and has existed in Our Dominion of Canada as and from the tenth day of September 1939.…

— W.L. Mackenzie King, Prime Minister of Canada, By Command, to Ernest Lapointe, Attorney General

RIGHT TO VOTE IN CANADA
1934: All Inuit lose the right to vote

1930-39: Two federal elections held

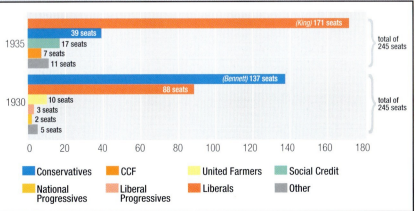

1935 (total of 245 seats):
- Conservatives: 39 seats
- CCF: 7 seats
- Social Credit: 17 seats
- Liberals (King): 171 seats
- Other: 11 seats

1930 (total of 245 seats):
- Conservatives (Bennett): 137 seats
- Liberals: 88 seats
- United Farmers: 3 seats
- National Progressives: 2 seats
- Liberal Progressives: 10 seats
- Other: 5 seats

1930–1939

1940 - 1949

1940 Women in Quebec granted right to vote

1940 Unemployment Insurance Act passed

When Canada entered World War II, Mackenzie King was determined to prevent a repeat of the Conscription Crisis of WW I. He promised a policy of "not necessarily conscription, but conscription if necessary." Compulsory service was instituted for many war industries and for "Home Defence," but not for military service overseas. However, as casualties in Europe grew and volunteer enlistment decreased, King found it impossible to maintain the required forces. He held a plebiscite on the question of conscription. Although a majority of French-Canadians voted "no," an overall majority of Canadians voted for conscription and King was able to proceed without the violent protests of WW I.

Changes influenced by the Depression continued to unfold. In 1940, women in Quebec finally won the right to vote. A federal Unemployment Insurance plan, which had been proposed by J.S. Woodsworth two decades before, was adopted in 1940. As well, the Rowell-Sirois Commission recommended massive changes to the federal powers.

In 1942, Conservative leader Arthur Meighen lost the Toronto by-election to a CCF candidate. Realizing that the party needed a leader to revitalize it, Meighen supported John Bracken, Liberal-Progressive Premier of Manitoba, to head the newly renamed Progressive Conservatives.

The CCF continued to do well, winning 39 seats in the Ontario election of 1943, making them the official opposition. In 1944, the Saskatchewan CCF under Tommy Douglas formed the first socialist government in North America. Nationally, the CCF led opinion polls in 1944, prompting King's Liberals to "borrow" many of the planks of the CCF platform: the "baby bonus" was instituted in 1944 and other social insurance measures were adopted.

After the bombing of Pearl Harbor, 22 000 Japanese Canadians were interned in camps in the interior of British Columbia and in Northern Ontario, or sent to work on farms in Alberta; their properties and businesses were also confiscated. In 1942, Alberta passed a law making it illegal to sell land to Hutterites or to "enemy aliens."

Attitudes about civil rights began to change after the war. Chinese and South Asian Canadians won the right to vote in 1947 and the Inuit and Japanese Canadians in 1949.

World War II had increased Canada's sense of power and responsibility. In 1945, Canada led by Lester B. Pearson, signed the United Nations Charter at San Francisco and, two years later, Canada was elected to sit as a member of the UN Security Council. A Canadian, John Humphrey, wrote the Universal Declaration of Human Rights. Pearson also represented Canada at the original meeting of NATO members in 1949.

THE WAR EFFORT

"Where a peace-time operation can efficiently carry on war-time work…it is in the best interests of the country to develop that peace-time industry for the purposes of the war rather than start a new enterprise, government-owned, for the same purpose.

We have used the powers indicated in the bill to dictate the prices at which people shall undertake work. We have gone into a plant and said, 'We want this article. The price is so much. You must manufacture that article….' We are getting to the point where, if a manufacturer has a thing which the government needs, we preempt it; we pay him what we think is a good price, and if he does not think so he has…an appeal to the courts."

— C.D. Howe, speech in House of Commons, 17 June 1940

▲ C.D. Howe, Minister of Munitions and Supply, transformed Canada into a major supplier of war supplies, from ammunition to tanks like that shown above.

◀ Canada's war effort campaign, 1942.

▼ The Wartime Prices and Trade Board was established at the beginning of World War II to regulate trade and inflation. The board was successful in keeping inflation under 3% from 1941 to 1945, well below WW I rates.

1940	1940	1940	1942
Canadian Congress of Labour endorses CCF as "political arm of labour"	National Selective Training and Service Act passed	Rowell-Sirois Commission Report released	Land Sales Prohibition Act passed in Alberta

"As soon as I put on my uniform I felt a better man."
— Tommy Prince

◀ Tommy Prince enlisted in June 1940 and became Canada's most decorated aboriginal war hero.

▼ Canadian soldiers captured Ortona, Italy, on 27 December 1943, after a week of fierce fighting and the loss of 1 300 soldiers. More than 45 000 Canadian men and women gave their lives in World War II in the fight for peace and freedom.

NATIONAL REGISTRATION

PUBLIC NOTICE IS HEREBY GIVEN that the National Registration Regulations, 1940 (as amended to February 1st, 1944), having the force of law, require:

1. THAT every person, in civilian life, resident in Canada who is sixteen years of age or over must be registered;
2. THAT all duly registered persons who change their address at any time after registering must within fourteen days notify the Chief Registrar for Canada of such changes;
3. THAT all duly registered persons who marry at any time after registering must similarly notify the Chief Registrar ...
   matrimonial status to the Registrar of the Mobilization Division in which he last resided before such change occurred).
4. THAT every registrant shall carry his registration certificate at all times;
5. THAT every registrant whose registration certificate has been lost, destroyed, worn out or defaced must obtain a duplicate certificate...

JAPANESE CANADIAN EXPERIENCE

NOTICE TO ALL JAPANESE PERSONS AND PERSONS OF JAPANESE RACIAL ORIGIN

TAKE NOTICE that under Orders Nos. 21, 22, 23 and 24 of the British Columbia Security Commission, the following areas were made prohibited areas to all persons of the Japanese race:—

LULU ISLAND (including Steveston)
SEA ISLAND
EBURNE
MARPOLE
DISTRICT OF QUEENSBOROUGH
CITY OF NEW WESTMINSTER
SAPPERTON
BURQUITLAM
PORT MOODY
IOCO
PORT COQUITLAM
MAILLARDVILLE
FRASER MILLS

AND FURTHER TAKE NOTICE that any person of the Japanese race found within any of the said prohibited areas without a written permit from the British Columbia Security Commission or the Royal Canadian Mounted Police shall be liable to the penalties provided under Order in Council P.C. 1665.

AUSTIN C. TAYLOR,
Chaiman,
British Columbia Security Commission

A Citizen's Voice

"Born in Canada…I had perceived myself to be as Canadian as the beaver. I hated rice. I had committed no crime. I was never charged, tried or convicted of anything. Yet I was fingerprinted and interned."
— Ken Adachi speaking of his internment, *Toronto Star*, 24 September 1988

◀ In February 1942, the government ordered the evacuation and internment of all Japanese Canadians living on the West coast. It affected more than 20 000 people.

"On December 7, 1941, an event took place that had nothing to do with me or my family and yet which had devastating consequences for all of us — Japan bombed Pearl Harbor in a surprise attack. With that event began one the shoddiest chapters in the torturous history of democracy in North America."
— Dr. David Suzuki, *Metamorphosis: Stages in a Life*

"I have to pay taxes, but have never been allowed to vote. Even now, they took our land, our houses, our children, everything. We are their enemies."
— Shizuye Takashima, *A Child in a Prison Camp,* 1971

▶ Japanese Canadians being relocated to camps in the interior of British Columbia.

"I see no reason why we should deal with the population of Japanese origin among us any differently from the way in which we deal with those of German and Italian extraction. If we deal with them differently — and we have done so — we do it in an account of racial prejudice."
— Angus MacInnes, Member of Parliament from British Columbia, 1943

1940–1949

1942	1942	1944	1947
Conservative Party changes name to Progressive Conservatives	CCF party, led by Tommy Douglas, win Saskatchewan provincial election	Family Allowances Act passed	Governor General given full power of Monarchy of Canada

EXPANDING THE SOCIAL SAFETY NET

UNEMPLOYMENT INSURANCE ACT, 1940

An Act to establish an unemployment insurance commission, to provide for insurance against unemployment, to establish an employment service, and for other purposes related thereto....

▲ A product of economic hardships of the Depression and the political and practical circumstances of WW II, the national employment insurance system became one of the pillars of the modern Canadian social welfare state.

FAMILY ALLOWANCES ACT, 1944

3. Subject as provided in this Act and in regulations, there may be paid out of unappropriated moneys in the Consolidated Revenue Fund from and after the first day of July, one thousand nine hundred and forty-five, in respect of each child resident in Canada maintained by a parent, the following monthly allowance:
   (a) in the case of a child less than six years of age, five dollars per month;
   (b) in the case of a child six or more years of age but less than ten years of age, six dollars per month;
   (c) in the case of a child ten or more years of age but less than thirteen years of age, seven dollars per month;
   (d) in the case of a child thirteen or more years of age but less than sixteen years of age, eight dollars per month:...

Speaking Out Against the "Baby Bonus"

"...Not only does the cash bonus for children threaten serious repercussions for the economies of the province and for the over-all welfare program...[i]t is also breeding an administrative octopus of fantastic proportions... [I]t strikes at the very basis of Confederation that precluded...the intervention of the central power and the threat of its officials into the civil life and homes of the citizens..."

— Charlotte Whitton, March 1945

▲ Charlotte Whitton would become mayor of Ottawa in 1951, the first woman in Canada to become mayor of a large metropolitan centre.

THE CANADIAN CITIZENSHIP ACT
Assented to 27 June 1946

...3. Where a person is required to state or declare his national status, any person who is a Canadian citizen under this Act shall state or declare himself to be a Canadian citizen and his statement or declaration to that effect shall be a good and significant compliance with such requirement.

"...For the national unity of Canada and for the future and greatness of this country, it is felt...that all of us, new Canadians or old, have a consciousness of common purpose and common interests as Canadians; that all of us are able to say with pride and say with meaning: 'I am a Canadian citizen.'"

— Paul Martin Sr. introducing the Bill on Nationality and Naturalization (which provided a legal definition of Canadian citizenship), 22 October 1945,

A Citizen's Voice

We are a people bounded on one side by the northern lights and on the other by an inferiority complex just as vivid, a people distracted by the mossy grandeur of the old world from which we came and by the power, wealth, and fury of our American neighbours. We are the last people to realize, and the first to deny, the material achievements of the Canadian nation, which all the rest of the world has already grasped and envied. Self-deprecation is our great national habit.

— Bruce Hutchison, "The Canadian Personality" CBC radio talk show, September 1948

CITIZENSHIP

▲ First Citizenship Ceremony, 3 January 1947. The Canadian Citizenship Act conferred common citizenship on all Canadians, whether they were Canadian born or not.

1947	1949	1949	1949
Saskatchewan Bill of Rights Act passed	Inuit and Japanese Canadians enfranchised	Property qualifications for right to vote eliminated	Supreme Court of Canada replaces Privy Council

NEWFOUNDLAND ENTERS CONFEDERATION

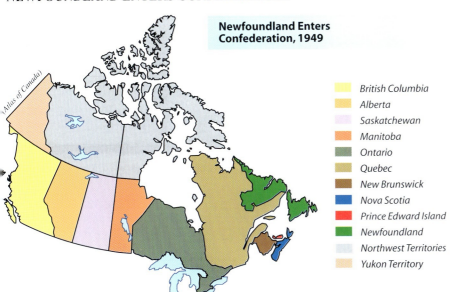

TOO LATE!
CONFEDERATION IS FOREVER
One Hour After We Enter Confederation
IT WILL BE TOO LATE
TO GET
The Greatest Good for the Greatest Number
ECONOMIC UNION WITH THE U.S.A.
The Minute We Enter Confederation
WE LOSE OUR RIGHT TO BARGAIN
BUT
UNDER RESPONSIBLE GOVERNMENT
We Can Always Have Confederation
After Six Months! Six Years! Anytime!
And
UNDER RESPONSIBLE GOVERNMENT
We Can Send a Delegation to Washington
We Can't Afford to Turn Our backs on
this Golden Opportunity
Vote Responsible—Send that Delegation

(National Library of Canada)

AN APPEAL

On Thursday, June 3, the toiling masses to Newfoundland will have the biggest and best chance they ever had in our country's 450 years history.

They will have the best chance they EVER HAD to make Newfoundland a better place for themselves and for their families….

Use this chance, fellow-Newfoundlanders….

Vote for Confederation.

Make June the 3rd the birth day of a NEW Newfoundland, a new Newfoundland fit for Newfoundlanders to live in.

Your sincere friend, *Joseph R. Smallwood*

Mr. Joseph Smallwood signing the agreement which admitted Newfoundland into Confederation, 11 Dec. 1948, Ottawa, ON.

▲ An intense campaign was waged in Newfoundland prior to a referendum on whether the province should join confederation or retain Dominion status.

▶ Newfoundlanders read about the results of the referendum. The confederates, led by Joseph Smallwood, won by a narrow margin, 52% to 48%.

(Canadian Heritage Gallery/NAC PA 128607)

"…In welcoming you as partners in the Canadian nation, we, of the rest of Canada, feel you are joining a good country — a country of which you will come to be as proud as we are. Canada is a country with a distinctive character and distinctive qualities.…"

— Louis St. Laurent address on the entry of Newfoundland into Confederation, 1 April 1949

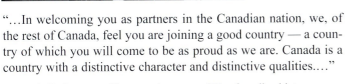

RIGHT TO VOTE IN CANADA
1948: The vote is extended to Japanese Canadians, the last Asian Canadians to receive the franchise

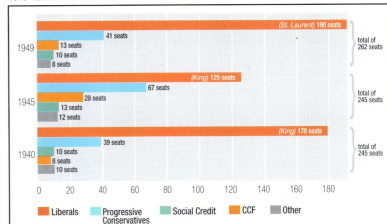

1940-49: Three federal elections held

1949: (St. Laurent) 190 seats, 41 seats, 13 seats, 10 seats, 8 seats — total of 262 seats
1945: (King) 125 seats, 67 seats, 28 seats, 13 seats, 12 seats — total of 245 seats
1940: (King) 178 seats, 39 seats, 10 seats, 8 seats, 10 seats — total of 245 seats

Liberals | Progressive Conservatives | Social Credit | CCF | Other

1940–1949

1950 - 1959

1950 — 28 Feb: Vincent Massey becomes first Canadian-born Governor General

1951 — Old Age Security Act passed

1951 — Thérèse Casgrain becomes first female leader of political party (CCF)

As post-war economic prosperity and the baby boom continued unabated throughout the 1950s, the Liberal government of Louis St. Laurent lengthened an unbroken string of election victories dating back to 1935. Inspired by leading cabinet ministers such as Lester B. Pearson, the Secretary for External Affairs, and C.D. Howe, Minister of Trade and Commerce, the Liberals expanded social welfare with measures such as Old Age Security. Immigration grew with the settlement of thousands of immigrants displaced by war in Europe, skilled workers needed in Canada's growing industries, and refugees from the 1956 Hungarian Revolution.

A sense of Canadian national identity continued to grow. In 1951, the Royal Commission on the Arts urged the government to provide broad support to the development of the arts and culture through the creation of the Canada Council. The next year, its author, Vincent Massey, became the First Canadian-born Governor General.

Human rights, which are largely a provincial responsibility, slowly began to be expanded in a piecemeal fashion. The Ontario government passed a Fair Employment Practices Act in 1951, and this was followed by the federal government's labour code in 1953.

Despite federal success, the Liberals had little impact at the provincial level, with the exception of the Atlantic Provinces. The Union Nationale controlled Quebec; the Conservatives held Ontario, the Liberal Progressives continued to govern in Manitoba, the CCF maintained power in Saskatchewan, and the Social Credit Party was unbeatable in Alberta and BC.

The longer the federal Liberals stayed in power, the more complacent they became. In 1956, they faced a corruption scandal and used closure to limit debate on a Trans-Canada Pipeline Bill. This event helped to swing public support away from the Liberals. In the election of 1957, the Progressive Conservatives, led by John Diefenbaker, won a narrow minority victory. A year later, Diefenbaker won the greatest majority to date, 208 of 265 seats. He appointed Ellen Fairclough to the Cabinet, a first for women. In Quebec, Thérèse Casgrain became the first female to lead a provincial party, the CCF.

LOUIS ST. LAURENT

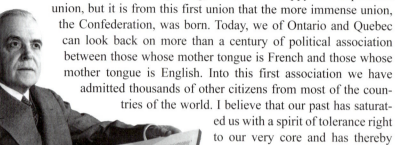

Our nation has another element of diversity because it is based upon the association of two races and two cultures. The political union of Upper and Lower Canada occurred in 1840. In the beginning, it was an unhappy and unpleasant union, but it is from this first union that the more immense union, the Confederation, was born. Today, we of Ontario and Quebec can look back on more than a century of political association between those whose mother tongue is French and those whose mother tongue is English. Into this first association we have admitted thousands of other citizens from most of the countries of the world. I believe that our past has saturated us with a spirit of tolerance right to our very core and has thereby given us the exceptional potential for understanding other nations and collaborating with them.

— Louis St. Laurent, speech, 27 March 1950

DEMOCRACY

In a true democracy the majority must not use its power as a steam roller riding ruthlessly over the interests and feelings of the minority; while, at the same time, the minority has an equal obligation to respect and co-operate with the majority. Whatever democracy is, it is not government by brute force but by persuasion. It is a sense of fair play, of justice and sportsmanship in the highest sense of that term.

— George W. Brown, *Canadian Democracy In Action*, 1952

We are supposed to have a two- or three-party system in Canada, yet one party has been in office, with only two intervals, ever since 1896, and continuously since 1935. This has led one observer to speak of Canada as a one-party state, and to attribute the phenomenon to the skill of the Liberal party in representing the lowest common denominator of political opinion in a country with an unusual dispersion of racial, religious, and sectional interests....

— C.B. MacPherson, *Democracy In Alberta: Social Credit and the Party System*, 1952

Pipeline Debate Hits New Heights Of Bedlam

One of the most controversial debates in Canadian parliamentary history was provoked by a proposal to build a trans-Canada line for transporting petroleum and gas from Alberta to Eastern markets. The pipeline was to be built ...with government assistance and private enterprise [involving] an American company....Many politicians and Canadians were disturbed by the heavy American involvement.... The bill was introduced in the House of Commons in January 1956. [After] four months...the debate finally ended on May 25, 1956...when the Liberal government used a device known as "closure" to end any further discussion of the bill and ensure its passage. The bill was passed by a vote of 148-52 on June 6. Closure left a lasting legacy with the Canadian public.

— *Ottawa Citizen*, 26 May 1956

1951	1952	1956	1957	1958
Fair Employment Practices Act passed	Pearson elected President of UN General Assembly	Female Employee Fair Remuneration Act passed	Pearson wins Nobel Peace Prize	Canadian Broadcasting Act passed

JOHN DIEFENBAKER

"I am the first prime minister of this country of neither altogether English or French origin. So I am determined to bring about a Canadian citizenship that knew no hyphenated consideration…I'm very happy to be able to say that in the House of Commons today in my party we have members of Italian, Dutch, German, Scandinavian, Chinese and Ukrainian origin — and they are all Canadians."

— Prime Minister John Diefenbaker, 29 March 1958, from a speech in the Canadian Parliament

◀ Diefenbaker appointed Ellen Fairclough as first female cabinet minister and appointed James Gladstone as Canada's first Aboriginal senator, 1958.

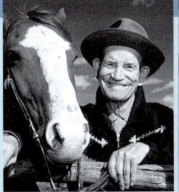

▲ In 1948 James Gladstone *(left)* was elected president of the Indian Association of Alberta. He was influential in dealing with federal government on initiatives such as the 1951 revisions to the Indian Act. Ellen Louks Fairclough *(right)* was elected to Parliament in 1950. She represented Canada at the UN, took part in several parliamentary committees, and became Canada's first female Cabinet Minister.

VINCENT MASSEY

…We are now spending millions to maintain a national independence which would be nothing but an empty shell without a vigorous and distinctive cultural life. We have seen that we have its elements in our history; we have made important progress, often aided by American generosity. We must not be blind, however, to the very present danger of permanent dependence.

— Excerpt, Chapter II, "The Forces of Geography," of the *Massey Report*, 1951

▶ Before his appointment as first Canadian governor general in 1952, Vincent Massey was appointed chairman of the Royal Commission on National Development in the Arts, Letters and Sciences in 1949. The ensuing report issued in 1951, known as the Massey Report, led to the creation of the National Library of Canada and the Canada Council. PM Louis St. Laurent *(right)* receives the report from Vincent Massey, 1951.

1950 – 1959

Does Canada Need a Governor General?

…Our constitutional set-up was neatly phrased by a former Governor-General, Lord Alexander, who described himself as "the monarch's shadow in Canada." As such, the Governor-General is our head of state, our first gentleman, the man who in his official person symbolizes Canada and all Canadians. He is also commander-in-chief of our armed forces, the fountainhead of Canadian honor, justice and mercy, and the figurehead in whose name the government of the country is carried on.

Some critics say no one should hold such a high office on appointment rather than on election but as Mr. Massey explained some years ago: "It is the only element which stands above all controversy, all partisan differences, and it makes of our national unity a living thing."

…[W]hile we are in the field of bold innovation, perhaps…our next Governor-General [should] be sought not among the ranks of diplomats, politicians, soldiers or businessmen, but among the real leaders of this age of nuclear fission and space travel — our scientists…

— *Star Weekly Magazine*, 19 July 1958

RIGHT TO VOTE IN CANADA
1950: Inuit become eligible to vote

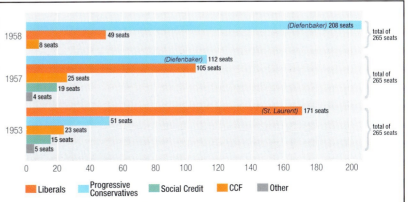

1950-59: Three federal elections held

1960 - 1969

1960 Quiet Revolution begins

1961 NDP created (formerly the CCF)

1962 Ontario Human Rights Code passed

The 1960s witnessed an explosion in demands by Canadian citizens, both old and young, for a more "just society." Fuelled by undreamed of affluence and a need to break away from the conformity of the 1950s, Canadians were no longer willing to accept the status quo.

A growing sense of Quebec nationalism swept Jean Lesage to power on the slogan "maîtres chez nous." During the "Quiet Revolution," Quebec's focus was on gaining economic and political control. This new confidence intensified feelings of Quebec nationalism and made separatist ideas acceptable.

Passage of Diefenbaker's Bill of Rights in 1960 was followed by Ontario's comprehensive Human Rights Code in 1962. The last vestige of legal discrimination in voting was removed when First Nation people no longer had to give up Indian status and treaty rights to vote. The Royal Commission on the Status of Women, led by Florence Bird, had a significant impact on women's equality rights and gave rise to the National Action Committee on the Status of Women (NAC).

By 1962, Diefenbaker's appeal was waning as inflation and unemployment rose. Pearson's Liberals promoted policies of regional economic development, expanded social welfare, and established a Royal Commission on Bilingualism and Biculturalism. While the newly-created NDP, under the leadership of Tommy Douglas, made gains in the West, Réal Caouette's Créditistes (Social Credit) burst on the scene in northern and rural Quebec. As a result, two consecutive Liberal minority governments were elected in 1963 and 1965. During this period, progressive reform legislation — including Canada Pension Plan and National Medicare Program — was passed because the ruling party had to keep third party support in order to remain in office. The cost of the new social programs were shared by the federal and provincial governments.

The bitter debate over the adoption of a new Canadian flag, followed by the huge success of Expo '67, inflamed a sense of Canadian nationalism. Controversy also flared up when the separate military services were combined into the unified Canadian Armed Forces. Also controversial were many changes Justice Minister Pierre Trudeau made to the Criminal Code because, as he said, "the state has no business in the bedrooms of the nation." Birth control and homosexuality were no longer illegal and abortions could be legally obtained in hospitals.

In April 1968, "Trudeaumania" gave the Liberals a majority government. Prime Minister Trudeau invited Canadians to become more involved in decisions about the country. They did so with battles raging over civil liberties and language rights.

BILL OF RIGHTS

(Canadian Heritage Gallery/NAC PA 112659)

PART I: BILL OF RIGHTS

1. It is hereby recognized and declared that in Canada there have existed and shall continue to exist without discrimination by reason of race, national origin, colour, religion or sex, the following human rights and fundamental freedoms, namely,

(a) the right of the individual to life, liberty, security of the person and enjoyment of property, and the right not to be deprived thereof except by due process of law;

(b) the right of the individual to equality before the law and the protection of the law;

(c) freedom of religion;

(d) freedom of speech;

(e) freedom of assembly and association; and

(f) freedom of the press...

"The right to vote is one of the great privileges of democratic society, for after all it is you the people, not the Gallup poll, who determine into whose hands the guidance of public affairs may be best entrusted."

— John G. Diefenbaker, 15 June 1962

Report on Bilingualism and Biculturalism, 1963

All that we have seen and heard has led us to the conviction that Canada is in the most critical period of its history since Confederation....decisions must be taken and developments must occur leading either to its breakup, or to a new set of conditions for its future existence...

A strong impression we drew from our contacts with thousands of French-speaking Canadians of all walks of life and of all regions of the country was the extent to which, for most of them, questions of language and culture do not occur in the abstract. They are rooted in the experiences of daily life.... They are inseparably connected with the social, economic and political institutions which frame the existence of a people and which should satisfy their many needs and aspirations.

A Citizen's Voice

...[A] thousand critics inform me that there is no such thing as a Canadian, no separate and distinct Canadian identity.

I am one.

Politicians and pundits assure me that there is no Canadian flag, no Canadian National Anthem, but I am content with our flag, a sort of red ensign with the Canadian coat of arms in the fly, and I am always moved when a good band plays "the Queen" but I could learn to stand up for "O Canada," too....

There are people like René Lévesque and Marcel Chaput who alternately assail me for oppressing my French Canadian brothers and threaten me with a promise to pull Quebec out of Confederation but I have been ship-mates with Johnny Bernatchez...kissed Ghislaine Gagnon and voted for St. Laurent and saluted George Vanier and cheered Jean Beliveau and I know they're Canadian too. We both learn each other's language and though their English and my French might be a bit shaky in spots, we're none the worse for that.

— T.B. Lamb, Editorial in *Daily Packet and Times*, Orillia, Ontario, 5 March 1964

1963	1963	1963	1964	1965
Commission on Bilingualism and Biculturalism	First election where vote is truly universal	FLQ begins bombing campaign in Montreal	Social Insurance Numbers introduced	15 Feb: Inauguration of Canada's new flag

RISING NATIONALISM IN QUEBEC

"We, the Liberal government, had just called an election on the nationalization of private power companies. A couple of nights later, a small group of us came up with the campaign slogan: 'Maitres chez nous' (Masters in our own home). The moment those three words rang out, the search was over. Even though instinct and common sense cried out here, potentially, was much more than a call for the takeover of a handful of private utilities."

— René Lévesque, Quebec Liberal Cabinet minister, 1962, cited in *To Be Masters in Own House in Canada: A Guide to the Peaceable Kingdom*, 1970

Maitre Chez Nous. C'est l'temps qu'ca change!
— Jean Lesage

▲ Jean Lesage was elected Premier of Quebec in 1960 on the promise that Quebec citizens would be masters in their own province. His "quiet revolution" modernized Quebec society by lowering voting age from 21 to 18, and taking control of medical services and education.

Front de Libération du Québec (FLQ), formed March 1963, set off some 200 bombs of increasing power during its seven-year terrorist campaign.

A NEW SYMBOL OF CANADIAN IDENTITY

▲ The resolution on the new flag was passed after some 308 speeches and six months of heated debate.

"This is the flag of the future, but it does not dishonour the past."
— Prime Minister Lester B. Pearson, House of Commons, 15 December 1964

"When someone tries to impose the Union Jack as our emblem, we do not agree, no more than we should accept the emblem of France and the French."
— Real Caouette, co-leader of national Social Credit Party, 10 June 1964

▲ Demonstrators crowded Parliament Hill as the Flag Debate began.

"…[A]t noon today…our new flag will fly for the first time in the skies above Canada and in places overseas where Canadians serve… There are many in this country who regret the replacement of the red ensign by the red maple leaf… [But] the patriotic motives that have led Parliament to adopt a new Canadian flag do not include disrespect for our past or the emblems of that past. (Translation) As the symbol of a new chapter in our national story, our Maple Leaf Flag will become a symbol of that unity in our country; …the unity that encourages the equal partnership of two peoples on which this confederation was founded; the unity also recognizes the cultures of many races…

Under this Flag, may our youth find a new inspiration for loyalty to Canada; for a patriotism based not on any mean or narrow nationalism, but on the deep and equal pride that all Canadians will feel for every part of this good land…"

— Lester B. Pearson, Inauguration of the National Flag of Canada, 15 February 1965

1960 – 1969

1966	1966	1967	1968
Munsinger affair: Canada's first political scandal	Pearson introduces Canada Assistance Plan (Canada Pension Plan)	Florence Bird appointed chair of Royal Commission on Status of Women	National Medicare Program established

THE PEARSON YEARS

▲ Pierre Trudeau, John Turner, and Jean Chrétien (who all went on to become Liberal Prime Ministers) with PM Lester B. Pearson in Ottawa, 4 April 1967.

Pearson: Father of a New Canada

...Lester Pearson...will be remembered as the architect of modern social democracy in Canada.

Pearson followed upon the social legislation of the past to create more of it in the present. He anticipated a potential Canadian democracy where each citizen would have maximum security in a political process geared to North American capitalism....Pearson built on the foundations of Canadian social security begun by King...

He leaves the Company of Young Canadians, a formal government agency, appealing to thousands of young people who don't want to be conformist, who don't want to be pushed into the sausage machines of big business and big government, but want to be involved personally and emotionally to help a needy, desperate world.

And he gave Canada, at long last, its own flag, the strongest symbol of nationalism any nation can claim.

— *Toronto Telegram*, 15 December 1967

EXPO '67

"We are witness today to the fulfilment of one of the most daring acts of faith in Canadian enterprise with an ability... Montreal has proven its capacity to carry through such an undertaking and its mayor has shown the inspired and dynamic leadership which was essential.

So have the people of Canada as a whole, through the cooperation of the three levels of government that was required...

Our...country's existence has always depended upon achieving unity of human purpose within the diversity of our linguistic and social backgrounds. Expo '67 offers perhaps the most striking proof ever assembled in one place that the future well-being of the whole community of man also depends upon achieving the unity of peace within the vast diversity of national policies."

— Lester B. Pearson, Opening of Expo '67, 27 April 1967

TOMMY DOUGLAS

▲ Tommy Douglas, considered the father of Medicare.

MEDICAL CARE ACT, 1966
Assented to 21 December 1966

...3. A contribution is payable by Canada to each province in accordance with this Act, calculated for each year in respect of the cost of insured services incurred by the province in the year pursuant to a medical care insurance plan of the province.

WOMEN TAKE A STAND

...I joined a chartered accountant firm with the degree of B.Comm. in Accountancy.... Seven days after my two years' registered service were completed I was told that my services were no longer required... [T]he partners felt that public accounting was no field for a woman, there was no spot in the firm for me.

— Letter from a young Quebec woman to *Chatelaine*, 1962

Women in the 60s took a more activist role on political and social issues that concerned them, from war to job discrimination.

I agree with you when you say that Medicare is too often thought of as mere "sickness insurance," and that our thinking should be directed towards "health insurance."...

Since 1962, when Medicare became a reality in Saskatchewan, there has been a tremendous increase in interest and activity in preventative medicine. Once the financial barrier between doctor and patient was removed, more emphasis could be placed on keeping people happy rather than merely treating them after they become sick.

For example, in many Saskatchewan centres we had the development of what are called community clinics.... An over-riding principle of these clinics is that people should be kept healthy, not merely treated after they become sick...

— Letter from Tommy Douglas in response to concerned citizen Mr. Foster, 25 January 1968

1968	1968	1969	1969
Quebec abolishes its Senate	New federal government White Paper on First Nation Issues proposes an end to Indian Act	Official Languages Act passed	Homosexuality and abortion liberalized

TRUDEAUMANIA

▲ Pierre Trudeau acknowledges the cheers of supporters after winning the Liberal leadership race. Trudeaumania swept the country during the election campaign, and he went on to win the 1968 election.

I have often been asked about...the phenomenon the press dubbed "Trudeaumania."... Almost everywhere I went, exceptional enthusiasm was apparent in the crowds that I found around me. People came in droves to rallies where I was speaking.... I had to believe...that the phenomenon was part of the spirit of the times. We had just come out of the Centennial celebrations; the year before had seen the remarkable success of Expo '67. The mood of the country was still one of festivity, and I happened to be there to profit from it. Of course, I wasn't about to complain!... What did I talk about in the course of my campaign? For the most part I spoke about the Just Society, about equalization payments, and about the Department of Regional Economic Expansion that I was proposing to create. I talked about language rights across Canada, about equal opportunity, and about the need for the government to protect the weak and to fight abusive speculators...."

— Pierre Elliott Trudeau, *Memoirs*, 1993

WHITE PAPER ON INDIAN POLICY

...To be an Indian is to lack power – the power to act as owner of your lands, the power to spend your own money and, too often, the power to change your own condition.... The Government believes that its policies must lead to a full, free and non-discriminatory participation of the Indian people in Canadian society. It requires a break with the past... The Government is...convinced that the traditional method of providing separate services to Indians must be ended. All Indians should have access to all programs and services at all levels of government equally with other Canadians....

— White Paper on Indian Policy, 1969

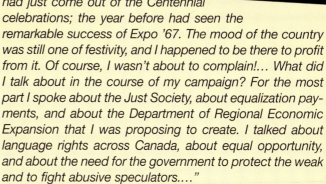

Jean Chrétien, Minister of Indian Affairs and Northern Development, meets with Aboriginal leaders. Chrétien's White Paper was, and continues to be, highly controversial.

A Citizen's Voice

...A lot of white people wonder why we want special status but they forget what we gave up. Our forefathers earned these rights and I want to make sure they are not lost... But every year they take away a little more. The Seaway chopped up our lands. They came and took our lands and when we said, "How much will we get?" they said, "We'll work something out." But they didn't take the white man's land when they could get ours — after all ours couldn't cost much, there was nothing on it but trees. But we like those trees....

— Mike Mitchell, "The Time for Singing is Past: An Indian Demonstration," *Weekend Magazine*, 19 April 1969

RIGHT TO VOTE IN CANADA

1960: The Indian Act is amended to extend the vote to Aboriginal Canadians living on reserves

1960–1969

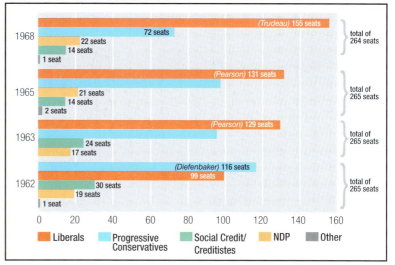

1960-69: Four federal elections held

1968: (Trudeau) 155 seats; 72 seats; 22 seats; 14 seats; 1 seat — total of 264 seats
1965: (Pearson) 131 seats; 21 seats; 14 seats; 2 seats — total of 265 seats
1963: (Pearson) 129 seats; 24 seats; 17 seats — total of 265 seats
1962: (Diefenbaker) 116 seats; 99 seats; 30 seats; 19 seats; 1 seat — total of 265 seats

Liberals | Progressive Conservatives | Social Credit/Créditistes | NDP | Other

1970 - 1979

1970
Oct: War Measures Act declared

1970
Voting age changed from 21 to 18

Politicians in the 1970s faced many continuing problems: inflation, labour discontent, and an increasing national debt. Federal and provincial bickering over division of powers and finances still festered. There was growing concern about Canada's dependence on the United States and fear of the increasing proliferation of nuclear weapons.

Pierre Trudeau's promise of a "just society" appealed to Canadians who believed that sweeping changes would make Canada a better place in which to live. His first real test as prime minister came with the 1970 October Crisis, when the separatist FLQ kidnapped British trade commissioner, James Cross, and later kidnapped and killed Quebec Labour Minister Pierre Laporte. Trudeau invoked the War Measures Act removing civil liberties from anyone suspected of supporting the FLQ.

In 1967, René Lévesque had left the Liberal government of Quebec to form the Parti Québecois. By 1973, the PQ was the Official Opposition. In November 1976, Quebec voters shocked the nation when they elected the first separatist government of Quebec. Within a year, the PQ government passed Bill 101 making French the only official language, replacing English as the language of business, and requiring families moving into Quebec to enrol their children in French-language schools.

The Trudeau government initiated many changes. In 1970, the voting age and the right to hold political office was lowered from 21 to 18. Women were appointed to key government positions and the Advisory Council on the Status of Women was set up in 1973. In 1974, the Election Expenses Act was passed to limit political party spending. The death penalty was abolished in 1976. Television broadcasting of debates in the House of Commons began in 1977. In 1978, Trudeau established the Canadian Human Rights Commission

First Nations, Métis, and Inuit communities pressured the Liberal government to address their concerns about social and economic conditions, and to begin to negotiate land claims and other treaty rights. In 1972, the Minister of Indian Affairs supported a National Indian Brotherhood proposal that became the blueprint for First Nations' control of their own communities. Métis organizations pressed their claims for recognition. The Inuit Tapirisat of Canada was established to protect Inuit culture, language, and land claims.

The 1978 Immigration Act finally ended the racist policies that had made it difficult for non-Europeans to settle in Canada. The multiculturalism policy had been proclaimed in 1971. Changes to the pattern of immigration throughout the decade gave the policy a new reality.

THE FLQ CRISIS

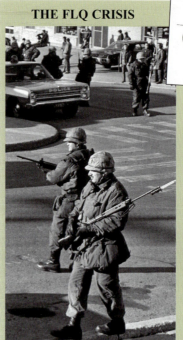
(CP PHOTO)

▲ Armed soldiers patrol a street in Montreal where British Trade Commissioner James Cross was reportedly being held. Mr. Cross was kidnapped by FLQ terrorists on 5 October 1970.

Ottawa outlaws FLQ to end terror reign
(The Spectator, 16 October 1970)

Mr. Prime Minister,

...the Quebec Government is convinced that the law, as it stands now, is inadequate to meet this situation satisfactorily.

...on behalf of the Government of Quebec, I request that emergency powers be provided as soon as possible... I request particularly that such powers encompass the authority to apprehend and keep in custody individuals who...are determined to overthrow the government through violence and illegal means....[W]e are facing a concerted effort to intimidate and overthrow the government and the democratic institutions of this province through planned and systematic illegal action, including insurrection...

— Robert Bourassa, in a letter to PM Trudeau, 16 October 1970

René Lévesque, leader of the separatist Parti Quebecois, yesterday issued an "urgent call" to all Quebeckers to organize against "repression" by police and troops conducting mass arrests across the province.

Lévesque told a press conference that citizens should band in their local communities, find out who is being arrested, help them obtain legal help and use any other democratic avenues to fight arbitrary government action....

— *Toronto Star*, 17 October 1970

GALLUP POLL OF CANADA: 87% APPROVE THE INVOKING OF THE WAR MEASURES ACT

— *Toronto Star*, 12 December 1970

Students in Calgary protest the invoking of the War Measures Act during the FLQ crisis in Quebec.

(Glenbow Archives NA-2864-6745)

1971	1971	1972	1973
Inuit Tapirisat of Canada (ITC) created	1 June: Federal Court of Canada established	Muriel McQueen Ferguson appointed first female Speaker of Senate	Federal Advisory Council on Status of Women created

ACTIVISTS AT WORK

Royal Commission on the Status of Women, 1970

Mandate: To inquire and report upon the status of women in Canada, and to recommend what steps might be taken by the Federal Government to ensure for women equal opportunities with men in all aspects of Canadian society.

Four Principles of the Commission:
1) women should be free to choose whether or not to take employment outside their homes
2) the care of children is a responsibility to be shared by the mother, father, and society
3) society has a responsibility for women because of pregnancy and childbirth
4) in certain areas women will, for an interim period, require special treatment to overcome the adverse effects of discriminatory practices …

— Report of the Commission, 1970

▸ Florence Bird was a broadcaster, journalist, author, and senator. In 1967, she was appointed Chair of the Royal Commissions on the Status of Women in Canada. Recipient of many awards, Florence Bird was made a Companion of the Order of Canada in 1971 and appointed to the Senate in 1978.

▲ Rosemary Brown was the first woman and the first black Canadian to run for the leadership of a federal party. She was first elected to the British Columbia legislature in 1972, sitting as a member of the NDP caucus.

"I am declaring as a candidate for the leadership of the Federal New Democratic Party. I am committed to a campaign in which there are no deals, where I will work hard and stay in until the end. My platform is based on a commitment to socialism, feminism, the preservation and development of our natural resources, the protection of the environment and for the rights of all workers and people."

— Rosemary Brown, Vancouver Press Conference, 12 February 1975

Human Rights
…It has become increasingly difficult for one to stand on the sidelines and merely watch the passing parade of human relations. There is no vacation period for those actively engaged in human rights…

Encounter
"People Participation" was evident and various groups, tenants and taxpayers alike were telling it — like it is for social action as never before.

The Garbage of History
"They brought the garbage trucks and moved us out of our community," one women [said] during "Encounter." The Community was Africville, a Black Community on the outskirts of Halifax.
Was the "Expulsion of the Africans" a blessing in disguise? I am inclined to believe that it was. As a result of this, every Black Community in Nova Scotia will remember Africville — and assess their status as citizens as it relates to Urban Renewal and Industrial Expansion…

History in the Making
I saw a new awareness on the part of many Black people…. [T]here is definitely a new breed of Black youth who cannot be denied. Their goals are well defined — dignity, self determination and respect. They are not in the majority but their ranks are growing….

— Carrie Best, *Pictou Advocate* 27 August 1970

▲ Carrie Best wrote the Human Rights column for the *Pictou Advocate* between 1968 and 1975. A recipient of numerous awards and a crusader for racial equality, improved conditions on native reserves, women's rights, and community development, Best worked well into her nineties.

▲ Dairy farmers throw bottles of milk at Minister of Agriculture Eugene Whelan in a protest against the federal government's refusal to provide subsidies for milk production, 3 June 1976.

1970–1979

1974	1974	1975	1975
Election Expenses Act passed	French becomes official language of Quebec	24 Mar: The beaver becomes Canadian symbol by Royal Assent	Wage and Price Controls introduced

MULTICULTURALISM

MULTICULTURALISM POLICY OF CANADA, 1971

…3.(1) It is hereby declared to be the policy of the Government of Canada to

(a) recognize and promote the understanding that multiculturalism reflects the cultural and racial diversity of Canadian society and acknowledges the freedom of all members of Canadian society to preserve, enhance and share their cultural heritage;

(b) recognize and promote the understanding that multiculturalism is a fundamental characteristic of the Canadian heritage and identity and that it provides an invaluable resource in the shaping of Canada's future…

A Citizen's Voice

…[U]niformity, where everyone "belongs," uses the same clichés, thinks alike, and behaves alike, produces a society which seems comfortable at first but is totally lacking in human dignity. Real unity tolerates dissent and rejoices in variety of outlook and tradition, recognizes that it is man's destiny to unite and not divide, and understands that creating proletariats and scapegoats and second class citizens is a mean and contemptible activity. Unity, so understood, is the extra dimension that raises the sense of belonging into genuine human life.

— Northrop Frye: *Bush Garden: Essays on the Canadian Imagination,* 1971

> "Freedom includes the right to say what others may object to and resent…. The essence of citizenship is to be tolerant of strong and provocative words."
> — John Diefenbaker, 9 April 1970

"The role that you fulfill is a vital one. With little more than dedication, enterprise and hard work, you have opened a two-way street for Ontario's society. It is largely through your efforts, and initially through your eyes, that New Canadians see their new homeland; and it is through the contributions of the respective groups that you serve that our Ontario society achieves its present richness and diversity. Whatever their origin, background and language, people find a home in Ontario."

— John Yaremko, provincial Secretary and Minister of Citizenship, at 20th anniversary celebration of The Ethnic Press Association of Ontario, 1971

▲ In 1970-75 the Canadian Immigration Policy was based on a points system. Sri Lankan applicants scored high in English and education.

NATIVES TAKE ACTION

▲ At an Ottawa meeting with PM Trudeau on 4 June 1970, Harold Cardinal (standing), leader of the Alberta Indians, asked that Indian treaties be settled by a "truly impartial claims commission appointed after consultation with the Indians."

INDIANS MARCH FOR FREEDOM

On October 27, here in Winnipeg, [a] Mass Protest March will be taking place… [T]he native people are… marching against…Racism, Poor Housing, Unemployment, Education, Exploitation, Degradation, Segregation, Oppression, Indian Act and Genocide. For: Human Rights, Social and Economic Equality, Political and Self-Government, Indian Nationalism, Religious and Cultural Reinstatement, Historical Recognition, Freedom, First Class Citizenship, Unity and Justice in a Just Society….

— "The Newspaper of the Native People," *The New Nation,* 23 October 1972

OUR WAY
The White Paper Policy

…The Just Society of the 60s emerged for Indian people, in blueprint form as the White Paper of 1969…. On grounds of equality and full participation, and describing Indian special status as discriminatory, it proposed abolition of our special constitutional position, repeal of the Indian Act, phasing out of the Indian Affairs Branch and ultimate assumption by Indian Bands of services, programs and responsibilities common to the national and provincial Canadian communities….

— *Saskatchewan Indian,* June 1975

1976	1977	1977	1978
14 July: Death penalty abolished	Bill 101 passed	Nova Scotia becomes the first province to enact a Freedom of Information Act	Immigration Act passed: reclassifying immigrants

ANTI-INFLATION ACT

▸ Trudeau implemented wage and price controls for a three-year period. Although the Act infringed upon the powers of the provinces, the Supreme Court of Canada declared in 1976 that Parliament had certain peacetime emergency powers and the legislation was therefore valid.

The harsh medicine worked. From a rate of nearly 11 per cent in 1975, inflation declined to 7.5 per cent in 1976 and 7.9 per cent in 1977… As I had feared, for imposing wage and price controls my government and I paid a heavy price in lost credibility. I know it cost me personally a great amount, because until then I think I was respected as a straight-shooting guy who told the truth as he saw it….

—Pierre Trudeau, *Trudeau Memoirs*, 1993

QUEBEC ELECTION, 1976

November 15, 1976, will always be an important date in Canadian history, but ten years from now it may be seen as a turn for the better, not for the worse…. Quebec has not yet voted to separate. It is unlikely ever to do so, unless it is told it is not welcome in Canada, unless its people are given the impression that to be French is to be a second-class Canadian.

The Parti Quebecois favors separation but its leader made it clear: separation would be decided by a special referendum, not by this election….

Exciting days are in prospect. Vigorous confrontations will develop. Confederation will be challenged, but challenges can be very constructive.

— *The Lethbridge Herald*, 16 November 1976

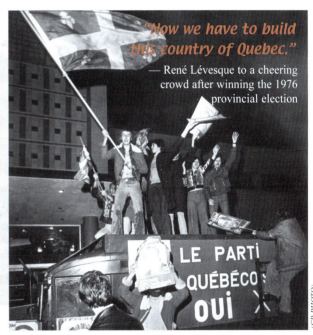

"Now we have to build this country of Quebec."
— René Lévesque to a cheering crowd after winning the 1976 provincial election

▲ Party supporters celebrate PQ election victory, Montreal, 15 November 1976.

TELEVISED DEBATE — 1979 ELECTION CAMPAIGN

Televised debate during the federal election campaign between party leaders (L-R): Ed Broadbent (NDP), Pierre Trudeau (Liberal), Joe Clark (PC) 13 May 1979, Ottawa.

"The politician will be only too happy to abdicate in favour of his image, because the image will be so much more powerful than he could ever be."
— Marshall McLuhan

"Having no Hollywood, our politicians are our stars."
— Roy MacGregor, Canadian Columnist

RIGHT TO VOTE IN CANADA
1970: The voting age is reduced from 21 to 18

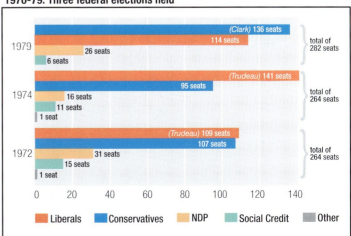

1970-79: Three federal elections held

1979: (Clark) 136 seats; 114 seats; 26 seats; 6 seats — total of 282 seats
1974: (Trudeau) 141 seats; 95 seats; 16 seats; 11 seats; 1 seat — total of 264 seats
1972: (Trudeau) 109 seats; 107 seats; 31 seats; 15 seats; 1 seat — total of 264 seats

Liberals ■ Conservatives ■ NDP ■ Social Credit ■ Other

1970–1979

1980 - 1989

1980
14 Apr: Jeanne Sauvé appointed first woman Speaker of the House of Commons

1982
17 April: Patriation of Constitution

ONE HUNDRED YEARS AFTER it was first sung, "O Canada" was finally made the national anthem on Dominion Day, 1 July 1980. Two years later, Dominion Day was renamed Canada Day. These symbolic changes further cut Canada's official ties with its British past. Of much greater significance was the patriation of the Constitution on April 12, 1982. The Canada Act, passed by the British Parliament, gave Canada full powers to pass its own Constitution Act, ending the requirement that Canada's constitution be amended in London.

In 1980, over 40% of Quebecers voted for "sovereignty association" in the first referendum. The "Non" side won on Trudeau's promise of constitutional reform. When the First Ministers' deal to patriate the constitution was finally struck without the agreement of René Lévesque, the Quebec National Assembly refused to ratify the constitutional resolution.

Equality for women continued to improve in other more symbolic ways. The battle over the Charter of Rights, especially the inclusion of the "notwithstanding" clause, led to constitutional recognition of equal rights for women. In 1980, Jeanne Sauvé became the first female Speaker of the House of Commons; in 1983 she became the first female Governor General of Canada. Bertha Wilson became the first woman appointed to the Supreme Court of Canada in 1982. Seven years later, New Democrat Audrey McLaughlin became the first woman to head a federal political party in Canada. In 1985, a change in the Indian Act ended discrimination against Native women who had married non-Aboriginal men. Racial equality also took a step forward when Lincoln Alexander was appointed Lieutenant Governor of Ontario in 1985.

In 1987, Prime Minister Mulroney attempted to strengthen Canadian unity by agreeing in principle, along with the First Ministers, to the Meech Lake Accord. Its primary purpose was to bring the province of Quebec into Canada's Constitution. It failed to become law because Manitoba, in a dramatic last-minute battle by Elijah Harper on behalf of First Nations peoples, failed to ratify the agreement, and Newfoundland withdrew its support.

In 1988, the Quebec government used the "notwithstanding clause" to pass a new language law after the Supreme Court of Canada ruled that Bill 101 was unconstitutional. At the same time, the Reform Party emerged to represent Western interest in Ottawa.

At the close of the 1980s, Mulroney's Conservatives won the election of 1988 with a reduced majority, and Canadians were vigorously protesting the proposed Goods and Services Tax.

CANADA'S NATIONAL ANTHEM

O Canada!

(English)
O Canada! Our home and native land!
True patriot love in all thy sons command.
With glowing hearts we see thee rise,
The True North strong and free!
From far and wide, O Canada,
We stand on guard for thee.
God keep our land glorious and free!
O Canada, we stand on guard for thee.
O Canada, we stand on guard for thee.

(French)
O Canada! Terre de nos aïeux,
Ton front est ceint de fleurons glorieux.
Car ton bras sait porter l'épée,
Il sait porter la croix.
Ton histoire est une épopée,
Des plus brillants exploits.
Et ta valeur, de foi trempée,
Protégera nos foyers et nos droits.
Protégera nos foyers et nos droits.

— Official Lyrics, 1980

Today the ethnic press is no longer a bootleg operation. It is respected and recognized with some of the glory falling on ethnic editors who, not long ago, were ignored....

— Stan Zybala, Editor, *Glos Polski (Polish voice)*, 1981

QUEBEC REFERENDUM, 1980

THE QUESTION:
"…do you agree to give the government of Quebec the mandate to negotiate the proposed agreement between Quebec and Canada [sovereignty association]?"

THE RESULTS		
NO	59.56 %	2 187 991
YES	40.44 %	1 485 821
Voter turnout: 84.3 %		

RENÉ LÉVESQUE'S LOSS
Serenity with a touch of anger

— Susan Riley, *Maclean's*, 26 May 1980

▲ On 20 May 1980, for the first time in the history of Canada, a province voted on whether to leave Canada. The vote divided families and friends. *(Above)* Supporters of the YES side.

(Bureau du Québec à Toronto)

▶ A disappointed René Lévesque on hearing the results. Later, PM Trudeau promised to "renew" Confederation.

1982
4 March: Bertha Wilson becomes first woman Justice of Supreme Court of Canada

1982
Dominion Day renamed Canada Day

1982
Quebec refuses to accept repatriation of the Constitution

1982
Canadian Charter of Rights and Freedoms takes effect

PATRIATION OF THE CONSTITUTION

▲ Larry Pierre, Okanagan Indian from British Columbia, one of 100 Indians who walked out of the First Nations Constitutional Conference, 1 May 1980, demanding Indian participation in the Constitutional talks.

◂ Queen Elizabeth II with PM Trudeau signing the Constitution, 17 April 1982, Ottawa.

"Today, at long last, Canada is acquiring full and complete national sovereignty. The Constitution of Canada has come home. The most fundamental law of the land will now be capable of being amended in Canada, without any further recourse to the Parliament of the United Kingdom… We now have a Charter which defines the kind of country in which we wish to live, and guarantees the basic rights and freedoms which each of us shall enjoy as a citizen of Canada. It reinforces the protection offered to French-speaking Canadians outside Quebec, and to English-speaking Canadians in Quebec. It recognizes our multicultural character. It upholds the equality of women, and the rights of disabled persons. It must however be recognized that no Constitution, no Charter of Rights and Freedoms, no sharing of powers can be a substitute for the willingness to share the risks and grandeur of the Canadian adventure. Without that collective act of the will, our Constitution would be a dead letter, and our country would wither away…

Let us celebrate the renewal and patriation of our Constitution; but let us put our faith, first and foremost, in the people of Canada who will breathe life into it…"

— Pierre Trudeau, Proclamation Ceremony, Ottawa, 17 April 1982

FIRSTS FOR WOMEN IN GOVERNMENT

▲ On March 1982, Scottish born Bertha Wilson was appointed Canada's first woman Supreme Court judge. In 1988 she wrote the important decision striking down Canada's abortion law.

"If women lawyers and women judges through differing perspectives on life can bring a new humanity to bear on the decision-making process, perhaps they will make a difference."

— Bertha Wilson

▲ Jeanne Sauvé at her swearing-in ceremony as Governor General in 1984. Sauvé was the first woman to serve as Governor General. She was also the first female Cabinet member from Quebec and the first woman elected as Speaker in the House of Commons.

▲ In 1986 Corrine Sparks from Nova Scotia was appointed first black woman judge.

"Although my beginnings were very humble, they were also very rich, because they gave me many things that money can't buy – a sense of security, a sense of identity and a sense of cultural connection. They also gave me the ability to dream."

— Corrine Sparks

1980 – 1989

1984	1985	1985	1987
2 Apr: The Young Offenders Act becomes law	Indian Act proclaimed	Lincoln Alexander becomes Ontario's first black Lieutenant Governor	3 June: Meech Lake Accord signed

MINORITY ISSUES

"Mr. Speaker, nearly half a century ago, in the crisis of wartime, the Government of Canada wrongfully incarcerated, seized the property, and disenfranchised thousands of citizens of Japanese ancestry. We cannot change the past. But we must, as a nation, have the courage to face up to these historical facts… I know that I speak for all Members on all sides of the House today in offering to Japanese Canadians the formal and sincere apology of this Parliament for those past injustices against them, against their families, and against their heritage, and our solemn commitment and undertaking to Canadians of every origin that such violations will never again in this country be countenanced or repeated."

— PM Brian Mulroney, House of Commons, 22 September 1988

Japanese Canadian Redress Settlement

"In achieving this redress settlement, the NAJC pays tribute to all Canadians who shared the Japanese Canadian dream of justice in our time…. The victory for justice and human rights is also a victory for the democratic process."

— Press Release from the National Association of Japanese Canadians, 22 September 1988

The Hamilton Spectator, Thursday, June 2, 1988: **Armed Indians set up blockades** — Grand chief heads to Ottawa for talks aimed at ending protest

▲ Incursions into what were considered native lands continued to be a source of conflict and negotiation during the 1980s. In the summer of 1990 conflict would escalate to an armed "stand-off" at Oka, Quebec when the town council announced expansion of a golf course on land that was an ancestral burial ground.

CANADIAN HEROES

◀ Marathon of Hope: 10-year-old Greg Scott walks with Terry Fox, 22, during his marathon run to raise money for cancer research. Both lost a leg to bone cancer.

"His courage heightened the world's awareness of the abilities of people with disabilities."
— Royal Bank ad, 1994

▶ Rick Hansen, a paraplegic since the age of 15, started the "Man in Motion World Tour" in 1985, completing it in 1987 after wheeling 40 000 km around the world.

WESTERN DISSATISFACTION

◀ Preston Manning, leader of the Reform Party of Canada, faces Joe Clark in the Alberta riding of Yellowhead in the 1988 federal election.

JURY STILL OUT ON REFORM PARTY

…dissatisfied Western Canadians have consistently indicated they want a better deal within Confederation. They are saying that by their rejection of the many fringe groups Canada could use a political vehicle that offers pragmatic solutions for the political problems and economic disparity in the federal system… And about 400 said it with their formation in Winnipeg last weekend of a new federal political party intended as a vehicle to take that discontent to Ottawa to force western issues onto the national agenda.

— *The Lethbridge Herald*, 3 November 1987

1987	1988	1988	1988
Reform Party created	Multiculturalism Act passed	Federal government enters into Free Trade Agreement with U.S.	21 Dec: Quebec uses the "notwithstanding clause" to override Supreme Court ruling

FREE TRADE PROTEST

▲ A group of demonstrators against Free Trade Agreement with the United States greet PM Mulroney outside a Toronto hotel, 20 September 1988.

LINCOLN ALEXANDER

▲ Lincoln Alexander congratulates Dr. Carrie Best after she was honoured by the Harambee Foundation in 1988. Mr. Alexander was Canada's first black Member of Parliament, first black cabinet minister in Joe Clark's government, and first black lieutenant governor, appointed in 1985.

MEECH LAKE ACCORD

"Meech Lake repairs the harm done in the 1981-82 constitutional negotiations when Quebec was left out. They called it 'la nuit des longues couteaux' — 'the night of the long knives.'"

— Bernard Roy, *Maclean's*, 20 March 1989

◀ In 1987, PM Brian Mulroney tried to end the bitterness between Quebec and the rest of Canada with the Meech Lake Accord. Key stumbling blocks were the "distinct society" clause for Quebec, the right of Quebec to have three out of the nine Supreme Court Justices, and the right to set its own immigration policy.

The Problem With Meech Lake
- 13% No Real Problem
- 3% All (Volunteered)
- 7% None (Volunteered)
- 9% No Opinion
- 11% Increases Power of Federal Government
- 12% Increases Power of Provincial Government
- 45% Increase Power of Quebec Government

(Decima Research)

"Meech Lake terrifies me..."
— Pierre Trudeau

RIGHT TO VOTE IN CANADA
1987: Judges become eligible to vote
1988: People with mental disabilities are granted the right to vote

1980-89: Three federal elections held

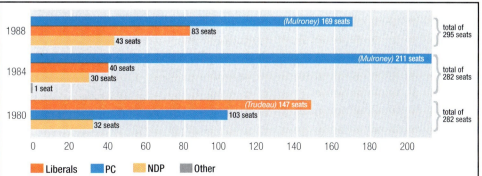

1988: (Mulroney) 169 seats PC, 83 seats Liberals, 43 seats NDP — total of 295 seats
1984: (Mulroney) 211 seats PC, 40 seats Liberals, 30 seats NDP, 1 seat Other — total of 282 seats
1980: (Trudeau) 147 seats Liberals, 103 seats PC, 32 seats NDP — total of 282 seats

Liberals ■ PC ■ NDP ■ Other

1980–1989

1990 - 1999

1990 — Andrée Champagne appointed first woman Deputy Speaker of the House of Commons

1990 — Meech Lake Accord rejected; Bloc Québécois created

THE 1990s WAS A DECADE of political firsts. After decades of negotiations, two Native land claims were settled. Kim Campbell briefly took office as Canada's first female prime minister before losing the 1993 election. Two attempts at constitutional reform were rejected, the Meech Lake Accord in 1990, and the Charlottetown Accord (in a national referendum) in 1992. The failure of Meech Lake led Conservative Cabinet Minister, Lucien Bouchard and eight other MPs to sit in opposition as a separatist party, the Bloc Québécois.

The Quebec desire for self-government came to a head in 1995 with a second referendum on sovereignty association. The 'Non' side eked out the narrowest of victories with 50.6% of the votes. Disparaging remarks directed at English and immigrant voters forced the resignation of Premier Jacques Parizeau and Lucien Bouchard became the new PQ leader and Quebec premier.

The Conservatives, led by Kim Campbell, suffered their worst defeat in Canadian history, losing all but two seats in the 1993 election. Jean Chrétien's Liberals came to power, winning mostly in Ontario and Quebec. Two regional parties, the Bloc Québécois and the Western-based Reform Party gained 54 and 52 seats respectively. For the first time, people with disabilities were guaranteed access to all polling stations and qualified people living outside Canada and prisoners could vote.

In 1990, the Ontario NDP under Bob Rae became the first socialist party to be elected in that province. Three years later, Catherine Callbeck became the first woman elected as a provincial premier when she led the Liberals to victory in Prince Edward Island. The federal New Democratic Party elected Alexa McDonough as its new leader in 1995 after losing all but nine seats in the 1993 election.

On an international level, the government was embroiled in fisheries disputes on both coasts. A dispute with the U.S over relative shares of the salmon catch in the Pacific Northwest lingered. The battle over protection of fish stocks on the Grand Banks led to the "Turbot War" in 1995 when Canadian officials boarded and seized a Spanish vessel outside of the 200-mile fishing limit.

Canadian judge Louise Arbour was appointed UN Chief Prosecutor for the International Criminal Tribunal for the former Yugoslavia and Rwanda. In 1997, she issued a warrant for the arrest of former Yugoslav President Slobodan Milosevic for crimes against humanity. Canadian diplomats were also active throughout the decade in getting most countries in the world to approve the establishment of a permanent international criminal court that would try people who commit crimes of war and crimes against humanity.

FAILURE OF MEECH LAKE ACCORD

"The main purpose of the Accord was formally to embrace the province of Quebec…aboriginal people are not against the right of Quebec to their own distinct society…

…In referring to the two "founding nations," the architects of the Accord neglected to acknowledge the equally legitimate place of aboriginal people within the Canadian nation. This was just one example of the way politics has always been used to silence aboriginal people…"

— Elijah Harper with Pauline Comeau, *No Ordinary Hero*, 1993

A Citizen's Voice

I am writing you to express my appreciation and support for your very principled stand on the Canadian Constitution, in general, and the Meech Lake amendments, in particular.… [B]oth documents should be superseded by a valid Constitution-making process which would come to grips with major issues such as a reformed Senate, the multicultural heritage and especially the status of Canada's Native peoples…

…The legitimacy of Quebec separation…was established…in 1980… This principle extends to any other province or territory.…

The second issue involves changing the Senate into a House of Regional Representation (the so-called Triple-E Senate). I…would prefer to have this body elected on a purely area basis…rather than a certain constituency of people. This would help compensate for the extreme population disparity across the…country.…

— Letter from William W. Zuzak to Premier Clyde Wells, Newfoundland, 3 June 1990

▲ As the deadline approached, the Accord had been ratified by the House of Commons and eight provinces. All First Ministers agreed to ratification, subject to further discussion. In Manitoba ratification required public hearings or unanimous consent of the Legislature. The Accord was scuttled when MLA Elijah Harper refused to grant consent. Premier Clyde Wells then declined to call for ratification in the Newfoundland Legislature.

CHARLOTTETOWN ACCORD, 28 AUGUST 1992

…The Constitution Act, 1867 is amended by adding…the following section:
2. (1) (b) the Aboriginal peoples… have the right to promote their languages, cultures and traditions and to ensure the integrity of their societies, and their governments constitute one of the three orders of government in Canada;
(c) Quebec constitutes within Canada a distinct society…
(d) Canadians and their governments are commited to the vitality and development of official language minority communities throughout Canada;
(e) Canadians are committed to racial and ethnic equality…
(h) Canadians confirm the principle of the equality of the provinces…

THE RESULTS
NO 54.3 % / YES 45.7 %
Voter turnout: 71.8 %

1990	1991	1992	1992
Oka conflict	Jan: Goods and Services Tax introduced	Charlottetown Accord: Canadians vote NO	Ontario lawyers vote against swearing oath to the Queen

ELECTION 1993

"Canada's first prime minister sought, unsuccessfully, to give women the vote. Today, a century after his passing, a woman stands before you as Prime Minister of Canada."
— Kim Campbell, address, Parliament Hill, Ottawa, 1 July 1993

◀ After a divisive leadership campaign, Kim Campbell led the Tories to a disastrous defeat.

The First Shall be Last
After two majorities, the Tories confront their rout as a party

…[T]he coalition that Brian Mulroney forged between the Western and Quebec Tories has been shattered. Nearly all its traditional constituency of free-market believers and small government advocates has bolted to the Reform Party…

…Reform's historic breakthrough underscores that a surging number of Canadians want their MPs to be more accountable, to show loyalty to those who elected them rather than to the party whose colours they wear…

— *Maclean's*, 1 November 1993

PRAIRIE VOTERS VENT ANGER BY VOTING REFORM, GRIT
— *The Lethbridge Herald*, 26 October 1993

TODAY'S MAN
JEAN CHRÉTIEN'S LIBERALS SWEEP TO POWER AS VOTERS RADICALLY RESHAPE THE POLITICAL MAP
— *Maclean's*, 1 November 1993

▲ Jean and Aline Chrétien acknowledge their supporters after the Liberal win is announced.

QUEBEC REFERENDUM

▲ Montreal Unity Rally, 27 October 1995. Citizens travelled from across Canada to support national unity.

"All those Canadians [who went to the rallies] can look at their children and say to them the next time the Canadian flag flies, they own a piece of it. They made a difference."
— Jean Charest, 1995

THE QUEBEC REFERENDUM QUESTION, 1995

"Do you agree that Quebec should become sovereign after having made a formal offer to Canada for a new economic and political partnership within the scope of the bill respecting the future of Quebec and of the agreement signed on June 12, 1995, Yes or No?"

THE VOTE

NO: 50.6%

YES: 49.4%

(Adapted from Maclean's, 6 November 1995)

A HOUSE DIVIDED
After a narrow No win, federalists fear that the real war is only starting
— *Maclean's*, 6 November 1995

Supreme Court ruling on secession won't affect PQ agenda."
— Lucien Bouchard, 1996

"The clarity bill goes some distance toward ensuring a democratic result. No longer could a valid secession question hide behind negotiating some other form of political or economic relationship, nor could it give a province merely a mandate to negotiate. Bill C-20 is a good piece of consumer legislation, defending the rights of voters to know exactly what they are buying at the ballot box."

— Editorial, *London Free Press*, 15 December 1999

1990–1999

1992	1993	1993	1993
Prison inmates get right to vote in federal elections	Jan: Catherine Callbeck becomes first woman premier in Canada	4 Nov: Sheila Copps becomes first woman to serve as Deputy Prime Minister	4 Nov: Joyce Fairburn appointed Leader of Government in the Senate

YOUTH PARTICIPATION

APEC PROTEST RAISES NEW QUESTIONS ON WHO'S DOING SPYING

…Last week, The Vancouver Sun reported on documents that revealed that the RCMP used informants to infiltrate and report on the activities of groups that were acknowledged to be non-violent protest organizations. The documents also revealed that the RCMP assembled dossiers on members of these groups, that high profile members were placed under police surveillance prior to the APEC conference, and that pictures of "potential troublemakers" from these groups were taken and circulated.

If these reports are accurate, they not only illustrate a shocking failure on the part of the RCMP to properly appreciate the nature and importance of the free speech and privacy rights of Canadian citizens. They also raise important questions about RCMP intelligence gathering…

— John Russell and Andrew Irvine, *Vancouver Sun*, 2 October 1998

▲ Demonstrators wait in the lobby of the Vancouver Police Station to file complaints over police brutality at a demonstration in Vancouver during a visit by PM Chrétien, 18 December 1998.

◀ Students from Appleby College in Oakville, Ontario, participate in a variety of community service, from clearing grounds at a local senior citizens' home to building a children's shelter in India.

> **"Canada's chief justice says the Charter of Rights and Freedoms has made the role of the courts more complex – and more controversial."**
>
> — Chief Justice Antonio Lamer, CBC Interview, 27 August, 1999

JUVENILE OFFENDERS

Canada treats young offenders cruelly enough

Contrary to the very powerful message delivered in Theo Moudakis' cartoon, Canada's young offenders do not receive a mere slap on the wrist for their misdeeds. Indeed, according to figures from the U.S. Department of Justice released earlier this year, Canadian young people are incarcerated…10 to 15 times as often as young Australians or young Europeans.…

— The John Howard Society of Sault Ste. Marie

ROLE OF THE COURTS

1996	1997	1998	1999
25 Apr: Maple tree officially proclaimed national arboreal emblem of Canada	Calgary Agreement confirms "equality of status" for provinces	Federal government issues formal apology to Native peoples for past injustices	1 Apr: Nunavut officially becomes Canada's third territory

A Citizen's Voice

For 47 years I was solely an American, now I am both an American and a Canadian. The first was my birthright, the second my choice. I love both countries. They share the same geography and much the same lineage...but they are governed differently: Canada's "Peace, Order and Good Government" feels safer to me, somehow, than America's "Life, Liberty and the Pursuit of Happiness." The first seems to want to gather its citizens together, and the second seems to want to spotlight its citizens separately. Maybe it's because I came of age in the American turmoil of the 1960s and 70s, amid Civil Rights battles, political assassinations, and the Vietnam War; but I don't feel at ease with the American mindset. It's too clear-cut, too black and white, too fundamentalist; American decisions about right and wrong come too easily. I'm more comfortable with the *messy middle of life* – grayed and relative and multi-faceted. Canadians compromise with difficulty, but I think they come closer to the ancient ideal of a "golden mean."

I now choose to live under a Canadian government...but I am grateful for my American birthright that let me choose my present, and my Canadian future that won't deny my past. I was born and raised an American, I am married to a Brit, and I am living as a Canadian. It's a blessed trinity!

— Carol Milne-Smith, journal entry, 27 April 1995

NISGA'A TREATY

The Importance of the Nisga'a Treaty to Canadians

"Back in 1967, the leaders of the Nisga'a Tribal Council came into my law office to ask me to sue the government of B.C. to obtain recognition of their Aboriginal title.... Now the Nisga'a are on the verge of signing the first modern treaty in B.C. history. Last November, by a vote of 70%, the Nisga'a people ratified the treaty. …

Under the treaty the Nisga'a will own 1,992 sq. km of land, approximately 8% of the Nisga'a traditional territory (at least two ranches in B.C. are larger). The Nisga'a are to receive $190 million in cash, paid over 15 years. The treaty also provides for Nisga'a entitlements to forestry, fishery and wildlife resources. The treaty represents a hard-fought compromise. The Nisga'a released their claim to ownership of most (90%) of their ancestral lands, and over time will give up their exemptions from income and sales taxation on current Indian reserves....

The lion's share of the cost of the treaty will be borne by Canada. More to the point, the federal government has the responsibility to complete this unfinished business; settlement of the claims of the First Nations is a national responsibility…"

— Thomas R. Berger, O.C., Q.C., Queen's University, 10 February 1999

▲ Celebrating the signing of the Nisga'a Final Agreement in Terrace, BC, 27 April 1999. The treaty was then ratified in the House of Commons on 14 December 1999, supported by all political parties with the exception of the Reform Party.

"We don't believe in special status for English or French. We don't believe in special status for aboriginals. We don't believe in race-based status of any kind. It's a formula for disaster."

— Preston Manning, Leader of the Reform Party 1999

RANKING CANADA'S PRIME MINISTERS

Great
1. William Lyon Mackenzie King
2. Sir John A. Macdonald
3. Sir Wilfrid Laurier

Near Great
4. Louis St Laurent

High Average
5. Pierre Elliott Trudeau
6. Lester B. Pearson
7. Sir Robert Borden

Average
8. Brian Mulroney
9. Jean Chrétien
10. Sir John S. Thompson
11. Sir Alexander Mackenzie
12. R. B. Bennett
13. John Diefenbaker

Low Average
14. Arthur Meighen
15. Joe Clark

Failure
16. Sir Charles Tupper
17. Sir John J. C. Abbott
18. John Turner
19. Sir Mackenzie Bowell
20. Kim Campbell

— Jack Granatstein and Norman Hillmer, *Prime Ministers: Ranking Canada's Leaders*, 1999

RIGHT TO VOTE IN CANADA

1992: Voting rights are extended to prison inmates

1999: Voting rights for all inmates challenged

Single member plurality systems…tend to exaggerate the parliamentary representation of the strongest party, to penalize the second party and to devastate the third parties whose support is thinly spread across the breadth of the country.

— Brian O'Neal, *Electoral Systems*, Political and Social Affairs Division, Parliamentary Research Branch, 1993

1990-99: Two federal elections held

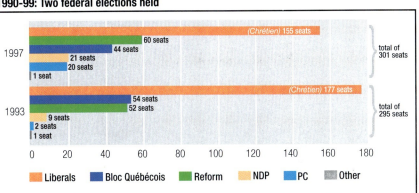

1997: (Chrétien) 155 seats; 60 seats; 44 seats; 21 seats; 20 seats; 1 seat — total of 301 seats

1993: (Chrétien) 177 seats; 54 seats; 52 seats; 9 seats; 2 seats; 1 seat — total of 295 seats

Legend: Liberals, Bloc Québécois, Reform, NDP, PC, Other

1990–1999

Into the 21st Century

CITIZENSHIP

Canadian civil rights under siege

Solicitor General Wayne Easter recently admitted that he is unable to discount the possibility that elements of the RCMP passed on information to the Americans that led to the deportation of Canadian citizen Maher Arar to Syria and the corresponding deprivation of many of his legal rights…

Modern political thought has seen an evolution from Hobbes leviathan-state, where individuals give over their liberties for social order, to a constitutional state… The great balancing act is to keep the state robust enough to protect and serve, but also to keep it from infringing on the rights of its citizens… Recall that after Sept. 11, 2001, Parliament approved sweeping new powers for the RCMP, allowing officers to search homes without warrants, arrest suspects without charges and gain access to a wider range of personal information…

Some tactics are violations of the Charter of Rights: individuals told that there are a number of unanswered questions about them and that they "ought to come in" but then officers won't speak to them if they bring a lawyer. Some tactics are sly and subtle; individuals visited by plainclothes (though clearly perceived by co-workers to be security officials) at work…

— Riad Saloojee, *Toronto Star*, 1 August 2003

▸ Mural protesting health care cuts, painted on a fence of former Wellesley Hospital site in Toronto, November 2002. In his report on the future of health care in Canada, Roy Romanow recommended a $15-billion cash infusion by 2006 for a sweeping expansion of medicare that would stop the growth of private medicine.

"Welcome home, Mr. Mandela."
— Claude Drouin, House of Commons

(Prime Minister's Office)

◂ November 2001: Nelson Mandela is proclaimed an Honorary Canadian in recognition of his human rights work and his struggle against apartheid in South Africa. The only other individual to be proclaimed an honorary citizen was Raul Wallenberg, a Swedish diplomat who saved hundreds of Jews during WW II.

CARING CANADIANS

(Lethbridge Herald)

Governor General honours city woman

It's a day Joyce Crittenden says she will never forget. Governor General Adrienne Clarkson presented her with the Governor-General's Caring Canadian Award…for her years of volunteer service with the Lethbridge Soup Kitchen.

"I never dreamed anything as lovely as this occasion would happen just by being a volunteer," Crittenden said after accepting the award…

— Caroline Boschman, *Lethbridge Herald*, 23 September 2001

◂ Roots of Empathy (ROE) is a program for school children aged 3 to 14. Each class "adopts" a baby who visits monthly with parent(s) and an ROE instructor. By interacting with the baby, students gain "emotional literacy" which helps them recognize their own feelings and understand how their actions affect the feelings of others.

"Our hope is to build a more caring, peaceful, and civil society, classroom by classroom."
— Mary Gordon, Founder/President, Roots of Empathy

Empathy key to just society

It's a question asked through all the ages: Of what is a just society made?

Socrates said it was giving all people their due. Others have pointed to compassion, respect for differences, or fairness. As prime minister, Pierre Trudeau called for the creation of a Just Society and said it would promote equality of opportunity. But when you seek the roots of these characteristics, you come to one thing: empathy – the ability to appreciate and respect the feelings of others.

— Cameron Smith, *Toronto Star*, 21 June 2003

"There was this 13-year-old boy whose mother had been murdered when he was four. Both his father and older brother were in jail…[he] had been in multiple foster care situations…One day…the boy held the baby…and that wise little baby snuggled right into this boy.… [He] rocked the baby…very quietly…[then] he asked the mother and the [Roots of Empathy] instructor:

'Do you think if nobody ever loved you that you could be a good parent?' "

— Mary Gordon, *The Changemakers Review*, June 2003

POLITICAL DIVIDE

There is in Alberta today a ferocious craving to be heard. The province's discontents keep multiplying without ever being debated, much less resolved. Central Canada's political elite has yet to accept the notion that westerners are anything more than bubbas in the boondocks, whose lives are consumed in envy of the lucky few plugged into action central in Toronto, Ottawa, and Montreal.... What [Albertans] will demand with increasing ferocity is greater control over their own destiny.

— Peter Newman, "Demanding to be Heard," *Maclean's*, 12 February 2001

Canadian parliamentary democracy, as it has evolved, places more power in the hands of the prime minister than does any other democracy, far more than the U.S. president wields, but more, too, than political leaders exercise in other parliamentary regimes.

— Jeffrey Simpson, *The Friendly Dictatorship*, 2001

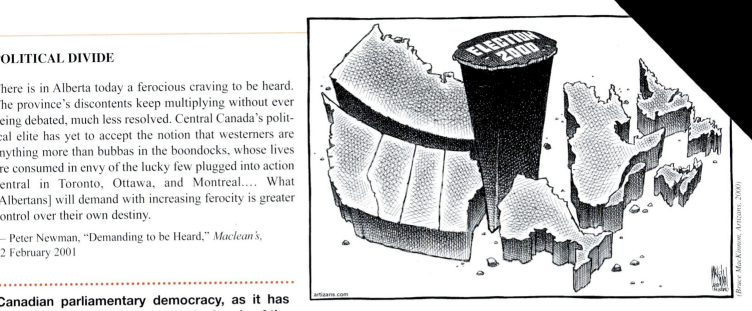

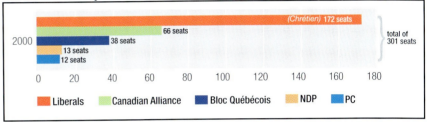

Into the 21st century: Federal election results

SAME-SEX MARRIAGE

Less than equal is less than adequate

Understandably, the current debate over the definition of marriage has elicited strong emotions. What's important is that this debate takes place in an atmosphere of respect. It's about equality, dignity and social justice. The government of Canada has referred draft legislation to the Supreme Court. This draft bill will recognize the marriage of same-sex couples for civil purposes while protecting freedom of religion.... Prime Minister Chrétien put it best when he stated that "there is an evolution in society."... The bill says, "Marriage for civil purposes, is the union of two persons to the exclusion of all others." But it also states, "Nothing in this Act affects the freedom of officials of religious groups to refuse to perform marriages that are not in accordance with their religious beliefs."...

— Martin Cauchon, Minister of Justice and Attorney-General of Canada, *Globe and Mail*, 19 August 2003

Canadians Conflicted on Same-Sex Marriage

— *CBC*, 4 September 2003

"He doesn't understand what it means to be a good Catholic. He's putting at risk his eternal salvation. I pray for the Prime Minister because I think his eternal salvation is in jeopardy. He is making a morally grave error and he's not being accountable to God."

— Bishop Fred Henry, 30 July 2003

Bishop's remarks upset colleagues

The Canadian Conference of Catholic Bishops is upset with Calgary Bishop Fred Henry for saying Prime Minister Jean Chrétien's soul is in jeopardy because of a federal draft same-sex marriage bill.

"It's not the sort of language that the rest of the bishops would employ," said Peter Schonenbach, the conference's general secretary... "My own stance on this and the stance of the bishops is that judgment is basically in God's hands and not in ours."

— *Red Deer Advocate*, 2 August 2003

Holding hands with the devil? Who am I to disagree...

I would like to say thank you to Calgary Bishop Fred Henry. His "burn in hell" warnings have made clear our rights as normal heterosexual, God-fearing people.

In my grandfather's day it was the right to discriminate against the Chinese. My father's generation discriminated against the Jews and I grew up with the N word on my lips. Now, thanks to the discriminatory and terrorist-like talk coming from the Catholic Church, I can rest easy knowing our children will have a class of people (gays and lesbians) that they can verbally abuse, deny rights to, beat, kill and even summon to hell for all time.

The Church has said they are sinners, the President of the United States has pronounced them all sinners, and if you feel or think any different, you'll spend eternity holding hands with the devil. OK, who am I to disagree.. Let the decimation and hatred continue.

— Tom Cattermole of North Vancouver, *The Providence*, 3 August 2003

Amery, L.S. 18
Anti-Inflation Act 37

B
Baby Bonus 24, 26
Balfour Report 18
Beliveau, Jean 31
Bennett, R.B. 20, 21, 22, 45
Bernatchez, Johnny 31
Best, Carrie 35, 41
Bilingualism and Biculturism
  Commission 31
Bill 101 34, 37, 38
Bill of Rights 30
Bill on Nationality and Naturalization 26
Bird, Florence 30, 32, 35
Bloc Québécois 42
BNA Act 18, 19
Borden, R.L. 14, 15, 17, 45
Bouchard, Lucien 42, 43
Bourassa, Robert 34
Bracken, John 24
British North American Act
  (BNA) 4, 5, 6, 8, 18, 19
Broadbent, Ed 37
Brown, George 7, 9, 28
Brown, Rosemary 35
Byng, Governor General 18

C
Callbeck, Catherine 44
Campbell, Kim 42, 43, 45
Canada Act 38
Canada Assistance Plan 32
Canada Council 28
Canada Day 38, 39
Canada Elections Act 17, 34
Canada Pension Plan 32
Canadian Armed Forces 30
Canadian Broadcasting Act 22, 29
Canadian Charter of Rights
  and Freedoms 5, 39, 44, 46
Canadian Citizenship Act 26
Canadian Congress of Labour 24
Canadian Human Rights Commission 34
Canadian Immigration Policy 35
Caouette, Réal 31
Cardinal Harold 37
Cartier, Sir George Etienne 6
Casgrain, Therese 28
Cauchon, Martin 47
CCF (Co-operative Commonwealth
  Federation) 20, 21, 22, 24, 26, 28
Champagne, Andree 42
Chaput, Marcel 31
Charest, Jean 43
Charlottetown 6, 42, 43
Chinese Immigration Act 14
Chrétien, Jean 32, 33, 43, 44, 45, 46, 47
Citizenship 46
Civil Rights 46
Clark, Joe 37, 40, 45
Clarkson, Adrienne 46
Confederation 4, 6, 7, 8, 9, 10, 11, 14, 15, 27
Conscription 16, 17
Conservative Party 11, 14, 15, 18, 25, 28,
  38, 41, 42
Constitution 5, 8, 38, 39, 42
Copps, Sheila 44
Crittenden, Joyce 46
Cross, James 34
Crowfoot 12

D
Dalton, Annie Charlotte 20
Death Penalty 37
Dennis, Jean Joseph 17

Department of External Affairs 15
Department of Indian Affairs 12
Depression 20, 26
Diefenbaker, John 28, 29, 30, 36, 45
"Distinct Society" 41, 42
Dominion Day 38, 39
Dominion of Canada 4, 6, 8, 9, 10, 11,
  14, 15, 21, 23
Dorion, Antoine A. 7
Douglas, Tommy 24, 32
Drouin, Claude 46
Duplessis, Maurice 20, 22

E
Election Expenses Act 34, 36
Elections Act 18
Electoral Franchise Upon Women Act 14, 17

F
Fair Employment Practices Act 28, 29
Fairburn, Joyce 44
Fairclough, Ellen 29
Family Allowances Act 26
Female Employee Fair Remuneration Act 29
Ferguson, Muriel McQueen 35
First Ministers' Conference 10, 13
First Nations 34
FLQ 31, 34
Fox, Terry 40
Free Trade Agreement 15, 41
Freedom of Information Act 37

G
Gagnon, Ghislaine 31
Galt, Alexander 6, 11, 15
Gladstone, James 29
Goods and Services Tax 38, 43
Governor General's Medal 24
Gray, John 20
Great Seal of Canada 8

H
Hansen, Rick 40
Harper, Elijah 38, 42
Head Tax 14
Henry, Fred 47
Homosexuality 33
House of Commons 11, 17, 34, 42, 46
Howe, C.D. 7, 24, 28
Humphrey, John 24
Hutchison, Bruce 26

I
Immigration Act 34, 37
Immigrants 36
Income War Tax Act 17
Indian Act 10, 12, 29, 33, 38, 40
Inter-Imperial Relations Committee 18
Inuit 34
Inuit Tapirisat of Canada 34, 35

J
Japanese Redress Settlement 40
"Just Society" 33, 34, 36, 46

K
Keynes, John Maynard 20
King, W.L. Mackenzie 18, 20, 22, 23, 24, 45

L
Land Sales Prohibition Act 25
Lapointe, Ernest 23
Laporte, Pierre 34
Laurier, Sir Wilfrid 10, 13, 14, 15, 45
League of Nations 14, 17
Lesage, Jean 31
Levesque, Rene 31, 34, 38
Liberal Progressives 28
Liberals 11, 13, 14, 18, 28, 33, 34, 41
London Conference 7, 8

M
Macdonald, John A. 6, 8, 10, 11, 13, 45
MacDonald, Mary A. 21
MacInnes, Angus 25
Mackenzie, Alexander 11, 45

Mackenzie, Bowell 45
Macphail, Agnes Campbell 18, 19
MacPherson, C.B. 28
Manitoba Act 10, 13
Manning, Preston 40, 45
Maple Leaf 31
Martin, Paul Sr. 26
Massey, Vincent 19, 28, 29
Massey Report 29
McClung, Nellie 14, 19
McGee, Thomas D'Arcy 7, 8
McLaughlin, Audrey 38
Medical Care Act 32
Medicare Program 32
Meech Lake Accord 38, 40, 41, 42
Meighen, Arthur 18, 24, 45
Mandela, Nelson 46
Metis 9, 10, 12, 34
Military Service Act 17
Military Voters Act 17
Mowat, Col. Oliver 18
Mulroney, Brian 40, 41, 42
Multiculturism 4, 34, 36, 41
Municipal Elections Act 14
Munsinger Affair 32

N
National Action Committee 30, 35
National Anthem 38
National Film Board 23
National Flag 1
National Indian Brotherhood 34
National Medical Program 30, 32
National Pension Plan 30, 32
National Policy 11, 18
National Progressive Party 18
National Selective Training
  and Service Act 25
Nationalism 30, 31, 32
NATO 24
Naval Service Bill 14, 15
NDP 30, 35
Nisga'a Treaty 45
Nobel Peace Prize 29
NORAD 31
North West Mounted Police 12
Northwest Rebellion 13
Northwest Territories Act 11

O
Official Languages Act 33
Official Secrets Act 23
Oka Conflict 43
Old Age Pensions Act 19
Old Age Security Act 28
Ontario Human Rights Code 30
Ontario/Manitoba Boundary Dispute 10, 12
Order of Canada 35

P
Pacific Railway Act 12
Paris Peace Conference 14, 17
Parliamentary Democracy 47
Parti Québécois 34, 37
Pearson, Lester B. 24, 27, 28, 29, 30,
  31, 32, 45
Person's Case 19
Pierre, Larry 39
Power, C.G. 23
Prince, Tommy 25
Privy Council 19, 27
Progressive Conservatives 25, 28
Progressives 18

Q
Quebec Conference 6, 8
Quebec Referendum 38, 43
Quiet Revolution 30, 31

R
RCMP 44, 46
Reciprocity 14, 15
Reconstruction Party 20
Red River Rebellion 9, 10
Reform Party 38, 40, 41, 43, 45
Refugees 34

Regina Manifesto 20, 21
Riel, Louis 9, 10, 13
Rogers, Norman 23
Romanow, Roy 46
Roots of Empathy 46
Rowell-Sirois Commission 22, 25
Royal Commission on the Arts 28
Rupert's Land Act 9, 10

S
Sabia, Laura 35
Same Sex Marriage 47
Saskatchewan Bill of Rights Act 26
Sauvé, Jeanne 38, 39
Schonenbach, Peter 47
Scott, Thomas 10
Sifton, Clifford 10
Single Men's Unemployed Association 20
Smallwood, Joseph 27
Social Credit Party 20, 21, 23, 28, 31
Social Insurance Numbers 31
Sovereignty Association 38
Sparks, Corrine 39
Special Status 33, 36, 45
St. Laurent, Louis 28, 29, 45
Status of Women 32, 35
Statute of Westminster 20, 21
Suffragists 17
Supreme Court of Canada 18, 20, 27, 36,
  38, 39, 41, 47
Supreme and Exchequer Court Act 11
Suzuki, David 25

T
Takashima, Shizuye 25
Thompson, John S. 45
Tilley, Samuel 7
Trudeau, Pierre 30, 32, 33, 34, 36, 37,
  38, 39, 41, 45, 46
Tupper, Charles 45
Turner, John 32, 41, 45

U
Unemployment Insurance Act 24, 26
Union Government 17
Union Nationale 20, 22, 28
United Farmers Party 18, 19, 20
United Nations Charter 24
United Nations General Assembly 29
United Nations Security Council 24
Unity Rally 43
Universal Declaration of Human Rights 24

V
Vanier, George 31
Versailles Peace Treaty 14

W
Wage and Price Controls 36, 37
War Measures Act 14, 16, 34
Wartime Elections Act 17
Wartime Prices and Trade Board 24
Washington Conference 17
Wells, Clyde 42
White Paper on Indian Policy 33, 36
Whitton, Charlotte 26
Wilson, Bertha 38, 39
Wilson, Cairine R.M. 19, 20
Winnipeg Equality League 17
Winnipeg General Strike 14
Wood, Henry Wise 19
Woodsworth, J.S. 22, 24
Wylie, Barbara 17

Y
Young Offenders 40, 45